The Paradox of Religious Secularity

KATHARINE T. HARGROVE, R.S.C.J.

Editor of the Proceedings of the College Theology Society

Prentice-Hall, Inc., *Englewood Cliffs, New Jersey*

Nihil obstat:
Very Rev. Msgr. William F. Hogan, S.T.D.
CENSOR LIBRORUM

Imprimatur:
✠ Most Reverend Thomas A. Boland, S.T.D.
ARCHIEPISCOPUS NOVARCENSIS

Newark, New Jersey, March 13, 1968

LIBRARY OF CONGRESS CATALOG CARD NO.: 68-24092

PRINTED IN THE UNITED STATES OF AMERICA

CURRENT PRINTING (LAST NUMBER):
10 9 8 7 6 5 4 3 2 1

Preface

Believe it or not, literary chemistry is a fact. Once you discover the reagent in any given group of manuscripts, amazing combinations and transformations take place almost automatically. That is what has happened in this present volume of the Proceedings of the College Theology Society.

The reagent I found in what Rabbi Borowitz thinks about "Confronting Secularity." As a result, if you compare the table of contents here with the program of the Thirteenth National Convention of the College Theology Society (Pittsburgh, March 26–28, 1967), you will observe the many changes brought about by this single shift of emphasis. In the event that you do not like the reagent I have chosen, there are countless others to stimulate your mind. All you have to do is track down the one most meaningful for you and then let it draw its own lines of force.

As it now stands, *The Paradox of Religious Secularity* is thematically focused on secularity. It adheres to the same general structure as its predecessor: by examining in context the biblical quotations[1] given after the part openings, you will be able to create exciting patterns of personal dialectic. A case in point is the scriptural key preceding Part V, "The Religious Phenomenon of Sex in a Secular Age." To understand the full import of what Judith actually replies to the elders of her people, you must flesh out the words of Ozias

[1] Quotations from the Pentateuch are taken from *The New Translation of the Holy Scriptures According to the Masoretic Text, First Section*, Philadelphia, Jewish Publication Society of America, 1962. All others are from *The New American Catholic Edition of the Bible,* New York, Benziger Brothers, 1961.

and the ancients by reading the Book of Judith. Then, and only then, will you grasp in a realistically new way the psychological insights and vital dimensions of the feminine mystique.

Judith in her time was a religious secularist who accepted the risk of autonomy. She reminds us that whatever the mystique presented to a human being, it is only by free choice, free decision, and free involvement in the human situation that a person realizes what it is to live in a divine milieu. "Hence, the norm of human activity is this: that in accord with the divine plan and will, it should harmonize with the genuine good of the human race, and allow men as individuals and as members of society to pursue their total vocation and fulfill it." [2]

The lines of force in a secular age need not make us fearful of any autonomy that is worthy of the name. This is the message conveyed, we trust, by every author on every page of this book. Hence, happy reading, and even happier thinking about what you have read.

KATHARINE T. HARGROVE, R.S.C.J.

[2] Pastoral Constitution on the Church in the Modern World, sec. 35, in Walter M. Abbott, S.J., ed., *The Documents of Vatican II,* New York, America Press, 1966, p. 233.

Contents

I Introduction

RABBI EUGENE B. BOROWITZ
1 Confronting Secularity 3

II Religious Commitment and Secularity on the Campus

REV. PAUL L. CIOFFI, S.J.
2 The College as Liturgical Community 19

MARY EILEEN PAUL
3 The Future of Eucharistic
Life in the College 27

LEONARY G. CLOUGH
4 The University Christian Movement 35

III Ecumenical Openings Toward Contemporary Secularity

MOTHER ANGELITA MYERSCOUGH, AD.PP.S.
5 Theology Courses in Catholic Colleges 43

RICHARD E. SHERRELL
6 The Department of Higher Education of the National Council of Churches 46

SISTER MARY PIERCE BUTLER, M.S.B.T.
7 The Relevance of Biblical Language to Theology 52

SISTER ALEXA SUELZER, S.P.
8 Theology of the Holy Spirit 60

ROSEMARY RUETHER
9 Two Types of Radical Theology 64

IV Ethical Crises of Development in a Secular Age

REV. DANIEL C. MAGUIRE
10 Modern War and Christian Conscience 75

M. RICHARD SHAULL
11 Confronting the Power Structures: Cooperation or Conflict? 92

REV. WILLIAM J. BYRON, S.J.
12 The Teaching of Business Morality 98

V The Religious Phenomenon of Sex in a Secular Age

PAULINE L. TURNER
13 The Contribution of Women to Theology 109

SISTER JANE STIER, O.S.U.
14 Women in the Church 119

EDWARD J. FOYE
15 The Androgynous Church 125

VI Religious Secularity

REV. JAMES J. MEGIVERN, C.M.
16 A Theology of Incarnationalism 145

SISTER M. REMBERT HUBING, O.S.F.
17 Theology and the Arts 160

REV. GERARD A. VANDERHAAR, O.P.
18 Theological Implications of Theories About the Universe 166

VII Conclusion

LESLIE DEWART
19 Autonomy: the Key Word in Secularism 177

Contributors 199

The Paradox of Religious Secularity

I Introduction

There was a famine in the land, and Abram went down to Egypt to sojourn there, for the famine was severe in the land.

GENESIS 12:10

RABBI EUGENE B. BOROWITZ

1 Confronting Secularity

Perhaps some members of the clergy can still avoid the question of religion's relationship to the secular style of existence. Clerical bureaucrats and local officiants may have their lives so fully integrated into their institutions that they can ignore or simply do not see what is moving in general society. The campus teacher of religion is too exposed to escape even if he teaches in a religiously oriented institution. He may hide from secularity, but it will come and seek him out. Something has happened—and that something seems irreversible.

The campus teacher of religion sees it most often in his students. They look at him differently from the way they used to. They listen, but not as they once did. There was a day when they regularly expected to be told what to believe. So we told them, and that generally satisfied them. If they asked questions on a subject that was not critical, they were satisfied to accept the answers given them. They had respect for authority and assumed that it had a legitimate role to play in their education.

That somewhat idealized picture of the past still holds true of many of our students, but they are no longer the mood-making group. Teachers today question student attitudes. They seem somehow too passive, too accepting. Can they really be mature if they do not assert themselves in argument, if they do not criticize and challenge, if they do not seek to exercise their autonomy?

For that is the key term for secular man: autonomy. He is determined to be a man for himself, to find his own way, to come to his own conclusions. That is why he looks and listens differently. He may be deeply determined to accept the guidance of religion, to recognize that it possesses a wisdom and competence that he can never own without its help. Still, he wants to take his personal resources as far as he can. As long as he can think, question, wonder, reason, he is not ready for authority. He wants explanations, analyses, validations, at least discussion. He does not want simply to be told the truth. He is not ready for conclusions until he has taken his search to the limits of his capacities, and perhaps not then. He knows he will almost certainly renew the quest tomorrow. Such decisions as he will make he considers private, highly personal matters; so only he, not another, may say when it is time for him to stop examining and make a commitment. Only he may say when and what he is willing to believe.

That is what autonomy means, and that is what secularity is teaching our children, youth, and adults. They have rights, real rights, in their study of religion as in anything else. More: insofar as we do not grant them their rights, they know us to have disqualified ourselves from teaching them God's truth. For though secularity may have taught them the fundamental necessity of the struggle for autonomy, it is clear to them, as it should be to us, that its foundation is already to be found in biblical faith. Each man is precious, for each man is created in God's image. Each man has capacities to understand and believe, and they are what dignify him as man. Each man has a conscience whose dictates he is bound to obey, even as he is responsible for sensitizing and informing it. Then, insofar as he strives to be what he was created to be, he must exert himself as best he can to appropriate what he finds to be the truth. Not to do so is to be less a man, even not a man, in both secular and religious eyes.

So our students today are skeptical where once they were accepting, and questioning where once they would have acquiesced. At their best they are active, not passive; self-determining, not conformist; independent, not subservient.

Of course, that is too great a burden for most of them. They aspire to autonomy, but they are afraid of its responsibilities; and they are probably also afraid of us and of some mythical power we may have to strike them dead. So they don that impregnable modern armament: politeness. They are respectful and courteous. They are quiet, but they do not thereby signify agreement. They sit with question marks behind their half-open eyes, wondering whether we really believe what we are saying, how we act when we are alone or with our peers, whether we can carry on a knock-down, drag-out argument with a well-informed skeptic. Regardless of what they answer on examination papers, who knows what they really believe?

They are increasingly a new breed. Though they may have been born in a faith and trained and nurtured in it, when they come to study it on a college level, they want to approach it with the same dispassionate, critical stance they bring to all their other serious study. That is how real religion's confrontation with secularity is, for secularity now sets the very tone and style in which the intellectual examination of religion itself must proceed. Even within a religious institution, where the body of students have almost certainly chosen the school because of its religious character; and even in its courses on its faith, including, as should be obvious by now, seminary courses in theology, the new secular skepticism makes itself increasingly felt. No wonder, then, that the college teacher who would ignore this growing change of mood must either have a chair at Shangri-la University or else have not faced anything but his research for several years. And at the secular university, what is masked elsewhere becomes the *sine qua non* of instruction.

Secularity often means a good deal more than a commitment to autonomy, and much of it takes forms far less positive than our students' desire to think religious questions through for themselves. Still, I have chosen to dwell on this desire at length because it is central to any discussion of secularity, and is the hidden agenda behind such current catch phrases as "The world has come of age," "God is dead," and "the post-Christian era."

If, then, religion in our time is to continue to say anything meaningful to large numbers—and perhaps we should recognize that at this moment we can speak in an authentic way to only a small minority—we must learn somehow to speak in terms of the secular style of our age.

Say what you will about the current confusion in theology, later ages will not be able to accuse any sizable minority of religious men of not seeking honestly, often radically, to grasp and respond to the meaning of what their society is going through. They may turn out to have been wrong, even foolish, but they will prefer that judgment to an accusation of the irresponsibility of inaction in an age seething with change and in a society marching to agnosticism or worse.

The first barrier to useful confrontation, then, is the willingness of religion to reach out to the secular style of our day. It would be difficult to see how it could not do so. That conceded, our problems, as usual, only begin. With whom shall we speak? And how can we do so? The questions sound so simple. The social and philosophic realities are annoyingly complex.

In organized religion, one can hope to find authorized spokesmen—though what once looked like carefully structured and defined faiths have in recent years shown themselves to be extraordinarily flexible and changing. Yet where shall one go if one wishes to open an ecumenical institute with contemporary secularity? The Communist Party certainly enshrines one aspect of it, and that was what made the exchange between Messrs. Roger Garaudy and Leslie Dewart so interesting. But western secularity is not only not essentially communistic; it may well be said to be postcommunistic. As long as communism was believable, there was a substitute absolute the irreligious man might accept. When the Communist god failed, that was the practical end of all absolutes and the beginning of postmodern secularist realism—the position that ideologies are per se bad, that final answers are unobtainable, that provisional responses to human situations are all we can hope for, that a healthy skepticism toward all human activities is the beginning of wisdom.

That is why I have kept referring to the secular style or mood of our age. It is not organized or socially structured, though it pervades our culture. To whom is one to talk, then, if one wishes to confront secularity? The answer must be: why, everyone who shares fully in our civilization, or, if we wish secularity at its best, those who lead our culture, whoever they are, and this is just our problem.

If there is any place where secularity is institutionalized, it is the modern university. Willy-nilly, it proclaims and empowers the secular style. Though its curriculum may contain no required courses on secularity, one of its most widespread activities is the conversion of its students to the secular approach to things. If that were altogether a bad thing, it would be the greatest argument known for complete education under religious auspices. But since the secular style, even from our religious standpoint, to a considerable extent is good and desirable, we cannot simply oppose it. Indeed, that is why, as our religiously sponsored universities pursue quality and high standards, they too must inevitably absorb much of this secular approach to things. And that is also why, as higher education grows in this country, we may confidently expect our society's commitment to secularity to increase.

The other place where we might hope to meet the significant secularities of our time is the loose confederation of persons, journals, and institutions that give leadership to our high culture, especially among our influential critics and writers.

However, whether our concern is to reach out to professors or to *litterati*, the distinctive response we may generally expect is: they are not interested. Particularly since the post-war revival of religion caused them to take another look, they are reasonably certain that religion has nothing to say to them. They aren't anticlerical or passionately atheistic—either would be a form of religious hangup; they just don't care. For them, not just God but religion is dead.

We face secular triumphalism, and that is why we should not be too optimistic about the results of whatever confrontation with secularity we might manage. The overwhelming majority of people find it as natural to ignore religious coffee houses, theological folk singers, and jazz liturgy as conventional religious activities. If our purpose in this outreach is to reverse statistics quickly and dramatically, then we are doomed to heartbreak and perhaps to a speedy return to religious reaction, a post-postconciliar stance, so to speak.

Realistically, then, our primary contact with secularity is likely to be in our students, particularly if we include all those who read and hear us as well as study with us. We shall confront secularity in the questions, the concerns, the criteria they bring to our discussions with them. That formal situation, however, imposes special burdens upon us with regard to recognizing our students' autonomy. The lecturer and his hearer are not equals. The audience must sit quietly and wait until the one side of a supposed communication between persons has run its course. Then the listeners are at best permitted a momentary statement or, more customarily, simply a question—and most of them must keep silent. Should they in their independence challenge the speaker radically, he has the height of his platform, the freedom from time limits, and the privilege of having the last word with which to overwhelm his challenger.

If that position of power is hardly conducive to treating one's audience as autonomous selves, how much more difficult it is for the classroom teacher, who is virtually omnipotent. He has maturity, advanced degrees, professional standing, examinations, and credits to use against his students, while he utilizes academic freedom and tenure to protect himself from review by the administration. And if he is a clergyman, he teaches with all the authority of his religion behind him.

What often happens, then, in this sinful world of ours is that when we do confront secularity, we meet it with power and not fair-minded intellectual receptivity. Yet if we violate the autonomy of our students in our teacher-student relationship, we cannot hope to validate our intellectual position. Only by exemplifying a willingness to confront the secular on mutually acceptable grounds—here, the autonomy of the individual—can we hope to accomplish anything in the realm of ideas. And since our students are perhaps sensitive to and suspicious of religious leaders beyond all others of the older generation, they are watching to see whether we will abuse our power.

Incidentally, this does not mean that they, in defense of their independence, want us to be their buddies or chums rather than their teachers. That would be as false to us as persons as it would be to the reasons which brought them to us. They seek us out, under the guidance of their institutions, as persons who are supposed to have superior wisdom or at least unusual competence in certain areas of intellectual concern. The gap in knowledge between us, they know, rightly grants us special status. That is why they come to us. What they ask of us is not pedagogic egalitarianism but only that we not exploit our power and deny them their rights as persons.

Given that insidious temptation behind us, how do we proceed to the intellectual task of confronting secularity?

Here our difficulties again multiply. For just as there is no unique institutional focus for secularity in our culture, so it has no agreed-upon intellectual content. It is apparently more a cultural mood than a single philosophic language. This is one reason that religious men spend so much time arguing about the true nature of secularity—the irony being that their debate is with other religious men. If, to take an easy example, Communist-style materialism spoke for modern secularity, we could devote our energies to understanding its terms. Then we would seek to translate religion into them wherever possible and question its assumptions where we could not.

Our greater difficulty is that today pluralism characterizes secular intellectuality as well as religious affirmation. Secularity can represent itself in atheistic existentialism or phenomenology or the philosophy of science or linguistic analysis; each has been proclaimed by some theoretician as the language *par excellence* of the modern world. In my opinion, the last-named orientation has proved the most exciting, perhaps because it is the most radical opponent.

If we could achieve an accommodation with linguistic analysis, it could clarify a significant if small area of a broad cultural experience; for that confrontation, because of its difficulty, might well turn out to be the touchstone of our success in meeting any secularity on the intellectual level. A number of notable starts have been made in this area. Though religion has not yet managed to cause any substantial retreats on the part of its antagonists, it has displayed a skill and a depth and, even more excitingly, a verve to inspire a certain hope for the continuation of the exchange.

Thus our responsibility is clear: we must know these various secular philosophies in all their appeal, and seek to meet their challenge in all honesty. Often, if we take the secular philosopher's rejoinders with full seriousness, we must admit that the issue remains in doubt or even that the arguments incline in his favor. We should not hesitate to admit this, to ourselves and to our students. Often such mental crosscurrents will help him by clarifying alternative criteria of judgment and different approaches to life. Religion then emerges in its distinctiveness, and the student may come to recognize that he too joins in the religious choice at these places of divergence, though other parts of his faith may well coincide with the conclusions of secular philosophy.

This leads us to another level of the confrontation. Religion cannot simply remain passive before the demands of a triumphant secularity. To see the encounter as religion's effort to explain itself in secular terms is to make of the older partner in the meeting a servile and dependent thing. Religion too is entitled to make its demands and ask its questions. It too must have autonomy, or else there can be no meaningful discussion. It must therefore issue its own challenges to secularist intellectuals. These challenges, I believe, should be primarily two in number. The first is directed toward the secularist's sense of certainty, and the second toward his approach to ethics.

Why are secularists so certain that what they define as making sense or being reasonable is the only proper way in which meaning can be considered meaning? The question arises because religious assertions are regularly asked to present themselves before the bar of secular categories of judgment and then are often told that they make no sense. Some religious men have struggled valiantly then to reinterpret religious teaching in such a way that it will qualify as meaningful within these restricted terms—I think of Braithewaite's lecture on "An Empiricist View of the Nature of Religious Belief" and, from a different standpoint, Leslie Dewart's *The Future of Belief*.[1] Others have sought to modify the secularist categories so that they will accommodate religious concepts better—Paul M. Van Buren's *Secular Meaning of the Gospel* and Pierre Teilhard de Chardin's *Phenomenon of Man* easily come to mind.[2] Yet the former efforts result in very substantial compromises with traditional faith, and the latter, despite the religious compromises, are generally rejected by secularist theoreticians.

Why should religious men not directly challenge any narrow concept of rationality, that is, any form which, by definition, makes it impossible or impractical for religious men to speak of their faith? Both "reason" and "rationality" have meant different things in different periods of philosophy. If historicism has made religious men humble about giving fixed and permanent objective statements of the content of their faith, it should equally keep philosophers from being dogmatic about the meaning of reason. And the con-

[1] R. B. Braithewaite, "An Empiricist View of the Nature of Religious Belief," unpublished paper (n.d.); Leslie Dewart, *The Future of Belief*, New York, Herder and Herder, 1966.

[2] Paul M. Van Buren, *Secular Meaning of the Gospel*, New York, Macmillan Company, 1963; Pierre Teilhard de Chardin, *The Phenomenon of Man*, New York, Harper & Row, Publishers, 1959.

temporary philosophic world is sufficiently pluralistic about what constitutes evidence and requires conviction so that the claims of one philosophic style cannot be asserted over religion without a serious challenge of the source of its own certainty.

The point of this religious counterquestioning of secularity is not to demonstrate the validity of religion. Rather, in exposing the dogmatic roots of the philosophy which stands against it in judgment, it may hope to clarify the common fundamental problems of religious and philosophic assumptions. By so doing, it may render what was the unequal contest of an outworn mysticism with a contemporary rationalism into a dialogue between two tentative, highly personal, and problematic efforts to search for significant truth.

Another area in which religion should take the polemic tack is the ground of ethics. It is the secularist's dearest hope that he can have the best of religion—ethics—without its faith in God or its institutional concretizations. The unethical conduct of religious men and institutions forms one of his chief weapons against religion's validity. He is, by contrast, happy to point out the many ethical men who are nonetheless atheists and agnostics. On both counts religious men have had to give humble assent. We have sinned, and others without our claims of faith have often been far more virtuous. Indeed, because of this prophetic secular judgment, we have resolved to be better, more active exemplars of our faith, and that has changed the complexion of contemporary religious life.

This should not deter us, as we look toward the future, from asking whence the secularist will derive his ethical impetus as the current tide of secularity swells to full strength. What doctrine or institutions will supply the kind of ethical motivation which will make men strive to be humane and will cause them to work and suffer to make their society more humane? For if religion is as hard-headed and realistic about secularity as secularity has been about religion, it is inconceivable that the secular world, as currently visible, can move significantly beyond moral neutralism. The intellectual bases for either a strong doctrine of natural law or some sort of Kantian moral law have been thoroughly eroded by modern skepticism. No philosophy today empowers and elevates conscience, while economics, sociology, psychology, and particularly psychoanalysis make us distrustful of it. If it is the personal on which we base our ethics, why should we care for persons, particularly if we are strong and able and they are weak and unattractive? And how can we have simple faith in man or the goodness of the interhuman when recent history has been one continuous revelation of man's unbelievable capacity for barbarism? Moreover, if man's perversity is so great and if his society is as dominated by self-interest and the will to power as we painfully have come to know, then it is not a little utilitarian accommodationism we require but tough, determined, unyielding devotion to the traditional moral values.

Again, the point of this counterthrust is not to prove religion right by showing the moral vacuity of contemporary secularity. In all such arguments leading to an either/or choice, the man who is convinced is as likely to take the "either" of nihilism to the "or" of religion. That is quite a risk indeed. The hope of this tactic again would be to deprive the secularist of his sense of superiority over religion, in the face of which meaningful discussion is most unlikely. If he can come to see that secularity might entail a loss of ethical substance and drive, he will at least be struck by his own problematic, which may then loom as great as religion's. And if he has firm faith in the fundamental signification of ethical action, there may be a basis upon which he and the religious man can begin to speak in common of the nature and direction of religious commitments. The quality of the discussion will then be altered, and perhaps will be made possible for the first time.

The temptation involved in such polemics is very great. Our audience, let us remember, is essentially the unsophisticated, the semireligious, if not the convinced. How easy it is for us to score before them victories against the heathen secularists. But if these refutations are quick and easy, if we win the day by flashy rhetoric or the exercise of clerical authority, we will have won nothing. For everyone will know that the opponent was not present, and that had he been, we might have been not simply less convincing but soundly rebuffed. If, then, our discussion is to be meaningful to our students, if we are to accomplish our task of confronting secularity through their struggle with it, we must treat it *particularly* in the absence of its representatives, with great respect. We must show an openness to its truths, a willingness to accept its criticisms, a knowledge of its arguments at their best, and only subsequently give our patient, thoughtful statement of opposition, followed in turn by a consideration of such replies to us as everyone knows would likely have been made. In stating our case, we must also give the opponent's as if he were present.

The issue now is less the substance of our confrontation than its style; and that, I am convinced, will be of more importance than what we say to those who listen to us. Two things are demanded of us to authenticate ourselves and our arguments. Both presume high intellectuality but go beyond it. They are realism and openness.

Our students will reject any public truth that contradicts a private reality. They are against all illusion, if they are moderns, and they will resent the use of sentimentality or nostalgia or an appeal to tradition as a substitute for argument. They know religion has been and is corrupt, while religious men have been and are full of doubt. They have been trained to face the glandular, monetary, class, and power realities of life. If we cannot face up to reality as modern men have increasingly come to know it, then religion is an escape and an abandonment of responsibility fit only for the weak and immature.

This does not mean that they want us to use obscene language or to revel in what the clergy has finally found out life is all about. They really would prefer that we know but then transcend these things in a way that shows the practicality of ennobling man—though not by evading or ignoring reality. Indeed, we validate the relevance and significance of religion when we show that its ideals apply precisely to the grimy, gritty world and not merely to the sanctuary or academy.

This is partly what is involved in openness, but the point must be taken somewhat farther. One of the astonishing discoveries of modern man is that the unthinkable alternative often turns out to have much to teach us. To close our discussion before a position has been thoughtfully examined has become a major methodological error. "There may be something to it." In the field of religion, discussion has often been prevented and foreclosed. What seems anathema or heresy, we have reasoned, should not receive consideration except at the hands of skilled polemicists. Our students expect far more of us. They will take it as a sign of insecurity in our own faith or thinking if we refuse to explore contrary possibilities and are not open to question, argument, and challenge.

Above all, they expect us to be open in recognizing our own limits and theirs. They know we do not know the whole of God's truth in final form, and they hope we know we do not know it all. They know that we may have enough faith to want to be pleasing in God's sight, but that our understanding of our faith in this complex, confusing age must surely have an open, questing texture. We too must be striving to know more and better what we believe. We too must have our questions and our doubts.

So we should be open to the fragile nature of their own web of commitments and denials of this moment. They too want to grow and develop, but they wish to do so in their own way. They want to come to faith autonomously. Hence they do not want to be rushed, pushed, manipulated, or catapulted. They want us to be open to their doubt and their quest, and they do not want us to force conclusions upon them. They therefore want, at the most, the climax of our instruction to be a question left with them for them to answer, without compulsion, in their own way. This does not mean, all the alternatives considered, that there is no room for us to state, even with some passion, what we consider to be true or what we believe our religion requires and why. Still, we must leave them with the right to decide. Even when pressing our views, we must respect their autonomy.

We teach to bring men to faith or to make them surer in it. They, the students of a secular world, study in order to have a basis for their own quite private commitments. We want converts, partisans, vocations. They want to hear as much as they can and in the quiet movement of their own souls make their decisions. We hope to convince. They study to consider.

That is the most poignant challenge of secularity to the teacher of religion, as it is to religion itself. Modern man insists upon his right to his own decisions. He will at best listen to us. Then, considering religion as one of many disciplines speaking to his soul, he will make up his own mind as to what he will do. He wants us, therefore, to state our faith as best we can, but then leave the issue of his decision with him in all openness. He will see—and that, from his point of view, is where our usefulness to him ends.

Can we be content to leave matters there, knowing full well that if we seek to do more than simply present our view, we will alienate him? How can we give our heart and soul and might to our faith and remain at peace if we do not finally bring the other to it? How can we leave the future of our belief in such a precarious state and not strive on until we have won another generation for what we believe is ultimately true?

The rise of secularity has, in fact, changed what we can hope to accomplish by teaching doctrine and how we may reach that new goal. Our intellectual formulations will at best make the autonomous decision for faith possible. In an age dominated by skepticism and negativism, this is no small accomplishment, particularly since, without that intellectual clarification, it is difficult to believe modern man could commit himself to anything. But insofar as religious faith has become a matter of the most personal, private decision, it will be far more affected by models than by argument. Here, who we are and what religion shows forth are the most effective means of making our impress on a secular world. Are we persons? Do we respect persons, even when we have power over them? Do we work and struggle and take risks for the fate of persons in our society and our world? These are the questions secular man is asking of us.

If we are frightened by the inadequacy of our theology and the insufficiency of our lives before this intense secular scrutiny, then let us remember that the destiny of religion is not in our hands. It is not we, as responsible as we must be, who must ultimately keep alive and sustain religious faith and institutions, but God Himself. It is because we trust in Him that we can face the anxiety of this new open-texturedness which the secular age demands of our teaching. It is because He has regularly chosen to use the simple and the ordinary as the instruments of His working that we can continue to try in our faltering way to serve His purposes. Without His help, how could we hope to do His work in this world? With His help, we may hope, in His own good time, to see even a world suffused with secularity become the place of His Kingdom.

II Religious Commitment and Secularity on the Campus

And because he put his trust in the Lord,
He reckoned it to his merit.

GENESIS 15:6

REV. PAUL L. CIOFFI, S.J.

2 The College as Liturgical Community

Speaking to the Society of Catholic College Teachers in 1964 on "The Constitution on the Sacred Liturgy and Prayer Life in the College," Father Gerard Sloyan made an important assumption which will be basic to our discussion of the future of eucharistic life in the university. At that time he stated:

> . . . I am assuming that colleges and universities conducted by the Church exist for the same general reason the Church does, namely, to pray: to offer fitting worship to God under the headship of Jesus Christ. The college, any college, is chiefly concerned with scholarship and teaching. This is what defines it, as distinct from a city council or day camp. . . .
>
> Just as the liturgy, chiefly the eucharistic action, is the *fons* and *culmen* of all the Church's activity, so the common prayer of a college is the test of whether her existence is justified precisely as Christian, precisely as Catholic, since so many things that go on in a Catholic college could be as well done elsewhere. . . . What a Catholic college can do is become a community of learners who are Christians, who learn precisely as Christians, who come to a summit of ecclesial activity and draw on a source of life in the sacraments they celebrate, as *this* Christian community. . . . [The] college does need to pray as a college—*collegium*—or it has no justifiable existence as a lesser community of that greater community, the Church.[1]

Without denying the specific academic role which belongs to the university *qua* university, Father Sloyan has defined it in terms of

[1] Gerard S. Sloyan, "The Constitution on the Sacred Liturgy and Prayer Life in the College," in *Proceedings of the Society of Catholic College Teachers of Sacred Doctrine, 1964,* Weston, Mass., 1964, pp. 107-122.

the ecclesial-sacramental reality of which it is a part. Do not underestimate the novelty of this approach. It is as much an innovation to define the Catholic university in these terms as it was to define our recovery of the mystery of the Church in terms of the eucharist. To call the Church the community of all those summoned by Jesus Christ to celebrate His eucharist in love is quite removed from the juridical perspective of the theology manuals, which left little room for the mystery of the Church and treated cult almost as peripheral.

Busy university administrators separated sometimes by a decade or more from the pursuit of theology may not have begun to see the Church in these terms, let alone the university. The specific academic nature of the Catholic university, which should not distinguish it from its secular counterpart, has almost totally overshadowed its fundamental cultic nature, which does distinguish it from the secular institution.

Ideally, the project of a Catholic university is a theological and cultic one, but in fact, theology becomes a subject relegated to the classroom and cult, a function to be executed in the university chapel.

Those who have begun to assimilate the teaching of Vatican II on the Church and the liturgy know that Father Sloyan's assumption is as sound as the theology on which it is based is solid. How can we help the policy-makers of the university relinquish the service-station concept of liturgy—masses, communions, confessions on the hour—for one of liturgy as the *fons* and *culmen* of the Catholic university's life, as the synthesis of the academic, administrative, social, and spiritual dimensions of the university community? To bring them to see this is a work of education, and as such will take time, tact, and imagination.

Setting up a model liturgical celebration supported by a solid catechesis, and attracting people almost on a person-to-person basis, may work in a small college community but will make almost no impression on a vast university complex; it will not influence the opinion of large numbers. This discussion is addressed to the liturgical life as it must be lived in the large Catholic university, with its complex of graduate and undergraduate schools and with the majority of students residing on campus.

For such a community, a much bolder and broader approach must be taken if the educative benefits of the liturgy are not to be lost to another generation of students and faculty. The entire populace of the university must be broached, from the rector-president to the faculty, the students, and the nonacademic staff.

I think the time is ripe for presenting to responsible university administrators a philosophy of education which sees the liturgy as the integrating and coordinating force underlying the Christian concept of education. Events have overtaken us, and administrators who may be hard put to justify their university as Catholic may be more open to such suggestions than we suspect. Let me explain.

In the context of the large and open Catholic university, the factors which once gave the university the Catholic stamp—at least, in the popular mind—are disappearing. Clerical domination is yielding more and more to active lay participation in university affairs. In the post-Vatican II era, we are becoming accustomed to an increased number of non-Catholic students and professors in our midst. The parents who select a Catholic university for their sons and daughters can no longer assume that the religious or clerical faculty will practice the close, almost familial supervision over its students as in times past. The specifically religious spheres are receding more and more—and this may not be a bad thing in itself. Obligatory chapel and retreats, for example, are no longer demanded, and who knows, even undergraduate theology requirements may be dropped. What is left to justify the university as Catholic?

True, it never was these things which gave the university its Catholic stamp; rather, the Catholic university's philosophy of education proceeded from a Christian anthropology. It was assumed that this vision would create an atmosphere which would permeate all the university's endeavors. One wonders whether the open and academically free Catholic university today has the channels and means by which to communicate its vision of man. One thing is certain: the service-station type of sacramental ministry is not sufficient to create that atmosphere or to communicate an integral Catholic world view.

A rich communal sacramental-liturgical life for students and faculty alike—and this is the thesis of the present discussion—can fill this void and once again give the university a sense of identity and mission. Thus can the university justify its existence as Catholic.

The eucharistic community may be only a small part of the total university body, but it can be the candle which sheds its light on and gives direction to all in the house. Here in community the groping student beset by serious doubts of faith can get some insight into what constitutes a Christian vision of reality; here he can see the sacramentalizing of the vision the Catholic university exists to give him.

What our students need more than any theology textbook or course or even individual sacrament is a community in which they can experience Christ loving and being loved. To justify our claim as Catholic, we will have to challenge their freedom with at least this. Our students need a powerful sign that Christ is alive and active in their midst, and that He is deeply concerned with human values. Only a community witness has such power. It is therefore through the eucharistic community that the university as such can and must assert its values, and this in a privileged form.

If the administrators of the university can be brought to see and share this vision, then the test of their sincerity will be their willingness to take the appropriate steps to achieve this goal.

Although the rector-president will be, in fact, the chief liturgist of the eucharistic community, he will need someone to execute the program for building up the community, coordinating its various phases and orienting all who will participate in the program—students and faculty, lay and clerical. He will need an administrator who is professionally competent in theology, liturgy, and Scripture, and who has a feel for religious psychology and a talent for organizing. What this coordinator or chaplain must do to build up the eucharistic community cannot now be presented in detail; it can only be suggested.

We have painfully come to see that the liturgy does not of itself create community, but rather presupposes it: the existing community structures are a phenomenon prior to liturgy. The coordinator will have to build on the clerical or religious community which administers the university, the students gathered around their dormitory or corridor chaplain, the members of a department, class, or club. He will need to study these small primary structures and determine how to aggregate them into a larger primary structure. The liturgical life of the clerical or religious group (if it has any) will have to be consolidated with that of the academic community. The coordinator will need to enlist the resources of the theology department. This does not mean, however, that the theology faculty should assume a pastoral role or use the academic structure as a vehicle for pastoral propaganda. It does mean that liturgical and sacramental theology must be effectively integrated into the program of undergraduate theology according to the spirit of section 16 of the Constitution on the Sacred Liturgy.

The co-ordinator will have to educate and elicit the collaboration of his clerical community. He will need to work closely with the clerical or religious prefects or counselors in the dormitory, who will be his links with the students. He will have to find forms and vehicles of communication to present his ideas to student leaders and lay faculty.

Essential to the program will be trained ministers, servers, and lectors; a choir and a choir director knowledgeable in traditional and contemporary music forms; a reserve of homilists who can handle the liturgical and biblical texts in a way which is relevant for a university congregation; and finally, a place of worship which by its appointments communicates to the congregation the peculiar character of Christian worship—worship in spirit and truth. Social vehicles will have to be found outside the cultic setting in which the mystery of Christian fellowship can be sustained and lived.

Such a program will hasten the day when the rector-president will assume his role as leader of the university community in the liturgical sense also. Then he will preside over the academic community gathered for worship, and stand within the corona of his concelebrating colleagues who reach out to embrace lay faculty and students, all freely consenting to their unity.

A celebration of this nature would be a sacralization of all the fields of human endeavor represented by the various schools—medicine, law, foreign service, business, liberal arts—and of the sacrificial scholarship which must go into them. Such a mass would tell the participants better than any university catalogue what they are doing at the university and who they are.

We may not yet have perfect liturgical forms (we never will here below), but we can have a liturgy which begins to reflect what Christ is trying to do with us now in the university situation. At a time when a humanism devoid of the transcendent is challenging genuinely supernatural values, the most valuable service the Catholic university can perform is to provide corporate witness. Its communal presence is a sacramental sign to the world of what it is and what its values are, a sign which is a solemn profession of its faith that God has intervened in history through the passion, death, and resurrection of Jesus of Nazareth.

When a true eucharistic community comes into existence, a natural dialectic will occur: reflection will translate itself into action, and experience will lead to deepened reflection. From the start, the community will have to question whether traditional forms meet its needs to worship God in spirit and truth in its particular situation.

The liturgical life of the campus will be marked in the future by an intensely ecumenical dimension. As we succeed in developing our own eucharistic community with the sense of identity this implies, it would be naive of us to ignore in our midst the existence of so many non-Catholic Christians both as individuals and as members of ecclesial communities. The open Catholic university is in fact an ecumenical community, and our ecumenical sensitivity must prompt us to find liturgical forms which can on occasion encompass these separated brothers in order to affirm our common values. The solemn inauguration of the academic year and the baccalaureate convocation are examples.

The presence of non-Catholic Christians among us must keep us aware that we are not the only eucharistic community on campus, but one of many. Ecumenical sensitivity and Christian charity will urge us to invite ministers of other denominations to serve the spiritual needs of students affiliated with them, and we will offer them fitting facilities for their worship. High priority in the development plans of the university should be given to an ecumenical center where theologians and students of various communions can meet for discussion, and a chapel where we can conduct non-eucharistic celebrations on Ash Wednesday, Bible vigils during Advent and Lent, the blessing and procession of the palms at the opening of Holy Week, and other sacramentals on feast days common to all Christian traditions. Intercommunion at this level would fill a real need for those who cannot yet feed on the one eucharistic bread. Altar set against altar challenges our charity and imposes on us an urgency to get on with our ecumenical task, using all the resources of solid scholarship that the university can provide to break down the walls of misunderstanding, prejudice, and ignorance.

What is the future of eucharistic worship at the university? No one can say for sure, but one thing is certain: experimentation will be essential. Permission for controlled experimentation is urgently needed. Without it, investigations go underground and become chaotic, closed, and capricious. Such exclusive eucharists are of no benefit to the Church at large and are in fact a contradiction.

Gently but firmly, we have to keep reminding the bishops of their own words regarding experimentation—I am thinking of sections 37 through 40 of the Constitution on the Sacred Liturgy—as *America* magazine has been doing in its editorials. On March 4, 1967, its editors wrote:

> . . . our liturgy, like most devotional practices, seems to smack more of Ellis Island than of Plymouth Rock. The times would appear right, if not indeed alarmingly late, to incorporate the great American experience into our style of worship. For (as the Constitution on the Sacred Liturgy expresses it, no. 37) the Church "respects and fosters the spiritual adornments and gifts of the various races and peoples." [2]

We can appreciate the fact that the bishops or the Holy See must be assured that experimentation does not mean anarchy, and that it will be in the hands of people competent in liturgical history and theology and capable of extracting perennially valid principles from timebound forms. Experimentation would demand a grasp of religious sociology, anthropology, psychology, art, and music. This is simply too much to demand of one or a few men. That is why the university is pre-eminently suited for the task of experimentation. New approaches must be presented to the bishops as the outgrowth of serious research and, of course, experience. There must be continual exchange between those guiding the experiments and the worshiping community. The whole program must be documented if it is to be of value to others. The resources of the theology department would naturally play an important role in this task.

We will have to devise forms which range from more structured Sunday eucharists to informal, intimate celebrations in the halls or dormitories. They must interpret the liturgical action well and need little or no interpretation themselves.

[2] "Liturgical Experimentation: II," editorial, *America,* March 4, 1967, p. 304.

The whole liturgy will need to be reworked into a non-Mediterranean, nonmonastic, nonagrarian idiom which looks to an urban and technological society and to worldly holiness. Only in this way will we succeed in creating a liturgy which does not give the impression that we are moving about in a world apart from the real one.

MARY EILEEN PAUL

3 The Future of Eucharistic Life in the College

As I understand it, "eucharistic life" is a more inclusive term than "eucharistic celebration." I would see the concept of "eucharistic life" as having dimensions as broad as the term "paschal mystery." The paschal mystery is defined in the Constitution on the Sacred Liturgy as Christ's "blessed passion, resurrection from the dead, and glorious ascension, whereby 'dying, he destroyed our death and, rising, he restored our life' " (sec. 5).[1] It is the mystery of Jesus Christ himself, the mystery of God's salvation which is spoken of so beautifully in Ephesians: "He has let us know the mystery of his purpose, the hidden plan he made in Christ from the beginning . . . , that he would bring everything together under Christ as head, everything in the heavens and everything on earth" (Eph. 1:9-10).

The paschal mystery cannot be limited to the eucharistic rite but includes every man and everything,[2] for "The Lord is the goal

[1] Constitution on the Sacred Liturgy, in Walter M. Abbott, S.J., ed., *The Documents of Vatican II*, New York, America Press, 1966, pp. 139-140.

[2] This universal aspect of eucharistic life as paschal mystery is clearly evidenced in the "Pastoral Constitution on the Church in the Modern World," which says: "But, linked with the paschal mystery and patterned on the dying Christ, he [the Christian] will hasten forward to resurrection in the strength which comes from hope." But it continues: "All this holds true not only for Christians, but for all men of good will in whose hearts grace works in an unseen way. For, since Christ died for all men, and since the ultimate vocation of man is in fact one, and divine, we ought to believe that the Holy Spirit in a manner known only to God offers to every man the possibility of being associated with this paschal mystery" ("Pastoral Constitution on the Church in the Modern World," sec. 22, in *ibid.*, pp. 221-222).

of human history, the focal point of the longings of history and of civilization, the center of the human race, the joy of every heart, and the answer to all its yearnings." [3] Indeed, in the light of the teaching of the Second Vatican Council, and in its profound and all-embracing Christological insight, one may say that where a man is, there is the paschal mystery lived, and that all real life is participation in Christ.[4] The eucharistic rite as we celebrate it, then, is the culmination and synthesis not only of Christian but of human experience.

I will understand the term "eucharistic life" to signify this broader dimension, the paschal mystery—Christ and human life caught up in him. By this I mean all of human life, especially in its present and in its presence in and for him, and not simply the ritual celebration of that life. For I believe the question of the future of eucharistic life in the college is not *simply* a question of renewal of rite. This statement is not intended in any way to indicate that reform of rite is not vital; on the contrary, it is absolutely necessary if we wish to speak to college students or to anybody else, for that matter. The eucharistic celebration seems to be dying on its feet on our campuses, in spite of our efforts to introduce variety within the permitted degree of experimentation, and in spite of heroic attempts to involve the students themselves in responsibility for their liturgy. Most often we do not have a living eucharistic celebration; rather, apathy and inertia seem still to characterize participation in rite. Re-form of rite, re-form of celebrants, and re-instruction of collegians in the congregation are all necessary to cure some of this apathy.

I would like to suggest, however, that in the broader perspective

[3] *Ibid.*, sec. 45, p. 247.

[4] So Paul VI in his closing address to the Council: "Consequently, if we remember, venerable brothers and all of you our children, gathered here, how in everyone we can and must recognize the countenance of Christ (Mt. 25:40), the Son of Man, especially when tears and sorrows make it plain to see, and if we can and must recognize in Christ's countenance the countenance of our heavenly Father—'He who sees me,' Our Lord said, 'sees also the Father' (Jn. 14:9)—our humanism becomes Christianity, our Christianity becomes centered on God; in such a way that we may say . . . a knowledge of man is a prerequisite for a knowledge of God" (Paul VI, "Closing Address to the Fathers of Vatican II," December 7, 1965, in *Catholic Messenger* [Davenport], February 24, 1966).

of eucharistic life as paschal mystery, we must have the courage to inquire about the eucharistic life of the college itself—its present and its presence, the dynamism of its now existence, the quality of its awareness, the meaning and kinds of human experience understood and happening there. Convinced as we are that all life is experience of the paschal mystery, we must look to ourselves as living paschal mystery to see why our liturgical celebration is only half-alive.

The first problem of the Catholic college is to define itself. This is no simple undertaking. Yet a deep sign of our awareness will be our conscious self-definition. Does the fact that our students experience our liturgy as peripheral and unessential not stem perhaps from the fact that we have not reflected sufficiently on our self-definition and the meaning of this for what we claim about our eucharistic celebration as central? A Presbyterian observer of our campus celebration wrote:

> The liturgy as presently performed in your chapel—leading from confession to salvation—will not serve as a tool of liberation nor an act of service for the sake of the public. It is turned in on itself, insisting that it is a conversation only for the communicants. Its pattern needs changing so that it expresses the Gospel as a given, with freedom as a consequence—all being done as a celebration for the sake of the public, which is where God's speaking/acting is taking place. . . .[5]

When we look at our liturgy to see what it tells us about our life, we have to ask ourselves who comes, and this leads us to the question, who *is* the college? Is it the administration, the faculty, the students? Our present liturgy or liturgies (one for students, one for religious faculty, and so on), give an ambivalent answer to that question.

What is our relation to the world and the Church? In defining ourselves, we must ponder this problem, and the attempt to solve it plunges us deep into the mysterious mutuality of world and Church. Father Gregory Baum, in a fine article discussing the relation of the Roman Catholic Church to other Churches, makes a useful distinction between the Church as institution and the Church as event:

[5] Rev. Jack Harrison, private letter to the author (n.d.).

> To regard the Church as institution focuses on one aspect of the mystery; another aspect is the Church understood as the communion or fellowship (*koinonia*) of the faithful produced by Christ. This second aspect is never static, canonically fixed and structurally solidified. It is always vulnerable to deformation by sin, and always subject to the saving and healing action of God in Christ as he shares his life with others in Word and sacrament.[6]

Father Baum goes on to say:

> . . . seen from the viewpoint of God's merciful and sovereign action, which uses institutional elements but is never dependent on or limited by them, a Christian community is more truly Church when it is more transformed into the people of God, into his family, into a spiritual brotherhood of faith and charity.[7]

In discussing the meaning of our Catholicity with colleagues, I discovered that they seemed to define the college's Catholicity in terms of institutionality. But as Father Baum points out, institution without event is empty. The event is the eucharistic life, the paschal mystery of Christ. In our effort to define ourselves and to discover just how eucharistic our life is, we must turn to the conciliar Church.

The Fathers saw the work of the Council as self-renewal, and they understood this renewal precisely as an entrance into the paschal mystery. This is what they announce in their opening *Message to Humanity*:

> Hence, obeying the will of Christ, who delivered Himself to death . . . , we as pastors devote all our energies and thoughts to the renewal of ourselves and the flocks committed to us, so that there may radiate before all men the lovable features of Jesus Christ, who shines in our hearts "that God's splendor may be revealed." [8]

The renewal is for the Fathers a deliberate entrance into a eucharistic life experience, as we have understood this term. For them the key word to describe this life is *service:*

> . . . faith, hope, and the love of Christ impel us to serve our brothers, thereby patterning ourselves after the example of the

[6] Gregory Baum, O.S.A., "The Ecclesial Reality of the Other Churches," in *Concilium*, vol. IV, Glen Rock, N. J., Paulist Press, 1965, p. 81.

[7] *Ibid.*, p. 82.

[8] *Message to Humanity*, in Abbott, *op. cit.*, p. 4.

Divine Teacher, who "came not to be served but to serve." Hence, the Church too was born not to dominate but to serve. He laid down His life for us, and we too ought to lay down our lives for our brothers.[9]

Following the example of the conciliar Church, the college too must enter courageously into the eucharist which renewal is, and be unafraid to meet and acknowledge the criticism of men like Pierre Berton, who says in *The Comfortable Pew*:

> "It is not an accident . . . that the most rapidly growing religious bodies in America today are those with the most grandiose pretensions to absolute rightness." When Christianity becomes part of the religious and social establishment, when it weaves itself into the national creed, it becomes an inflexible religion, suffering truly from a kind of "rightness" that renders it disdainful of new conditions. . . . It looks back upon the past rather than forward into the future, until it becomes itself fossilized, using symbols and language no longer appropriate to its place and time.[10]

To the degree that we as educators have become "inflexible" and suffer from "rightness," we are failing in our vocation to Christ. Berton compares the religion of the establishment, which "in today's society provides a cotton-wool haven for those who cannot face the kind of truths the Apostles had to face," with true Christianity, "which came into being as a difficult, dangerous, radical, uncomfortable, shattering, but also vastly stimulating and exciting way of life." [11] He shows that sociological and psychological studies reveal Christianity as hardening people in prejudice, class and social distinction, and the comfort of the status quo. Father François Houtart, commenting on the *Constitution on the Church in the Modern World*, asks, "To what have we reduced Jesus Christ? Have we made of the Church a world apart . . . almost an anti-world?" [12] And speaking of Christian institutions, he says:

> At a given time, the creation of Christian institutions was necessary, but now, some years later, their function is transformed. Created

[9] *Ibid.*, pp. 4-5.

[10] Pierre Berton, *The Comfortable Pew*, Philadelphia, J. B. Lippincott Co., 1965, p. 87.

[11] *Ibid.*, pp. 82, 83.

[12] François Houtart, *L'Église et le monde*, Paris, Éditions du Cerf, 1964, p. 20.

as a sign of the charity of the Christian community, they become little by little almost an exclusive service of this community . . . ; organized to give service to the collectivity, they become the instrument of the socially dominant class.[13]

It would seem that the Christian college—whatever else its Christianity might mean—should be characterized by an awareness of that "new humanism" which is the service proposed by the Council Fathers, and so by an openness to truth wherever truth is found. Indeed, such an institution should be farthest from a "cotton-wool haven," least characterizable as a form of corporate selfishness, a milieu cut off from actual life. Our institutions should be freest to investigate every sign of our times, every aspect of man's dynamic and challenging career, for we know there is nothing to be feared in the truth. For us, every truth is the face of Christ. We know the signs of the times are not a series of events in the past delivered in a set of revealed truths. They are what is happening in the present, happenings in which genuine novelty arises.

We are also aware that the search for truth is precisely a search. Insofar as we have thought we had all the answers, we have had neither answers nor questions. Berton's description of himself and his reaction to the Church may well be applied to our students and their reaction to us:

> I had seen some of the real problems that distress the human animal. My head was crowded with questions, ideas, vague longings, half-formed resolves, and some small troubles. Whatever it was I was seeking, I did not find it in that Church. Instead, I was subjected to a string of religious clichés which . . . was maddening to me. We were all about to enter a New Age; yet there was nothing in that service to indicate that the world was different, that communication was different, that men were different.[14]

We know that men are different. Houtart says, "Humanity has entered upon an era when change becomes the normal situation, and adaptation to change a basic value." [15] New questions are being asked, and new answers must ever be sought in a love constantly open to the ever-new revelation of Christ in this present world.

[13] *Ibid.*, p. 47.
[14] Berton, *op. cit.*, p. 9.
[15] Houtart, *op. cit.*, p. 54.

"Behold, I make all things new." How seriously we must take that statement! How alive we must be to be true to our Christianity!

This radical attitude should be reflected, for instance, in a creative curriculum. Does our curriculum reveal us as present to the creative center of our culture? Do we, in exploring curriculum possibilities, see ourselves as constituting not so much an institution as an event, as revelation happening to the students while they happen to us? Have we asked ourselves realistically the questions which are so forthrightly put in current educational journals? Are we "pace-setters, creating new patterns of teaching, of curriculum, of admission"? Do we "admit on an experimental basis groups of students who do not meet traditional admissions standards, or emphasize such 'nonacademic' criteria in selecting students as low socio-economic background . . . or a history of after-school employment"? [16]

How present are we to ourselves? Do we know the kind of student we teach and the world that each comes from? What are the value systems, the social-economic pressures that shape the lives of the students we teach? It is vital that we be aware of these to be effective teachers. Our effort must be to discover where the students really are and what their questions really are. But this places a heavy responsibility on us as a faculty. Each of us must be converted from complacency—the complacency, for example, of thinking we know Christ or that he is really central to our thinking, the complacency of speaking a language which is a tomb the risen Christ left long ago. How often our efforts to teach reveal to us that we are no longer asking real questions and, worse, no longer able to *hear* the real questions our students are asking. How present are we to each other as a faculty, as disciplines in interaction? How alive is our interchange with our colleagues? If we do not have a current grasp of other disciplines, how can we see their relationship to our own, and how can we be creative in exploring these relationships with our students?

How present are we to our immediate environment? Are we aware of educational needs we might possibly supply in service to our own community? And how imaginative are we in reaching out

[16] Roland H. Nelson, Jr., "An Admissions Man's Guide to College Organization," *College Board Review*, Fall, 1966, p. 18.

to the communities in the center of which we are? We can be certain that our students will not be servers of the community in a real and deep sense unless we as a college are.

I am proposing that we as Christian be an open institution, present to ourselves as ongoing event, present to the *present* of our students, our faculty, our immediate social community, our Church community, and the world. We should be alive to the challenges of education in our day, innovative and creative in exploring our fields. Like the Council Fathers, we must have the courage to examine the integrity of these very practical dimensions of our eucharistic life. We must discover the depth to which we are Christian, evidenced in the service and serving death of renewal. We cannot speak of apathetic students and indifferent faculty without inquiring to what degree we ourselves have created and foster this apathy and indifference.

If the central meaning of our being is the service we know to be Christ's passion, death, and resurrection, and if we are very clear on this eucharistic life of ours, then we will take risks for it, we will be generous and open-hearted and creative. Our life will be eucharistic in a deep sense, and it will be *Life*. I believe that in such an atmosphere we will have an alive eucharistic celebration, even given the obstacle of a partially revised rite, for I believe that our students will be genuinely coming to life, and we will be, too. And that life will be resurrection, and the dawning experience of our absolute future in Jesus Christ.

LEONARD G. CLOUGH

4 The University Christian Movement

At 10:28 P.M. on September 6, 1966, the University Christian Movement in the U. S. A. was born at McCormick Theological Seminary in Chicago, Illinois.

The founders stated in the preamble to the Articles of Operation, "The University Christian Movement will be a new chapter in a continuing history." Unless one views the formation of the UCM in that light, he cannot understand its full significance.

From the early days of the first American college, Christian students have gathered in voluntary associations to discuss matters of personal concern, to study and worship, and to plan ways of serving their fellow men within the academic, church, and political-economic communities.

In the second half of the nineteenth century, the inevitable happened: a student decided that it was time for concerned Christians in American colleges to meet one another in organized fashion for mutual enrichment, support, and service. Thus was born the intercollegiate Young Men's Christian Association, soon to be followed by the intercollegiate Young Women's Christian Association. For nearly three-quarters of a century, they were the major instruments of Protestant churches in this country encouraging discipleship among their students.

Early in the twentieth century, both Protestant and Catholic churches became aware of the need for establishing specialized ministries to Christian students on the campuses of state universities.

Thus were planted the seeds which flowered into intercollegiate Christian organizations like the National Newman Student Federation and various Protestant student Christian movements.

In 1944, a combination of pressures led to the formation of the United Student Christian Council—a federated structure for cooperative work in higher education—by the YMCA, the YWCA, and several Protestant churches. Among the notable achievements of the USCC were the development of strategies for cooperative work in state university campuses, the sponsoring of "ecumenical" conferences, and the provision of a body which could serve as the United States member of the World Student Christian Federation and as a "related movement" of the National Council of the Churches of Christ in the U. S. A.

Fifteen years later—in 1959—the need for a more unified Protestant approach to college campuses resulted in the creation of the National Student Christian Federation. Into this new creature were blended the former United Student Christian Council, the Student Volunteer Movement, and the Interseminary Movement. Although the identities of its constituent bodies were never completely submerged, the NSCF gradually found itself being transformed into a more effective, more ecumenical Christian community within American higher education. During this period, leaders of the NSCF and leaders of the two major Roman Catholic national student organizations, the National Newman Student Federation and National Federation of Catholic College Students, became personally acquainted and began to explore areas in which they had common concerns and goals. Similar explorations were made with representatives of the Orthodox churches in this country.

At the Seventh General Assembly of the National Student Christian Federation in September, 1965, it became clear that the time had come for basic changes in the NSCF's form and ways of work. Two of the most obvious reasons were that (1) denominational student movements were rapidly losing the loyalty and support of college students, and (2) many new groups of concerned students and faculty were emerging who wished to participate in a national ecumenical fellowship of Christians.

The Seventh General Assembly of the NSCF decided that the time had come to revise its constitution. It made provisions for the establishment of a special committee to work on this, and voted to permit the Central Committee to accept local groups as "provisional members" of the NSCF for one year.

During the academic year 1965-1966, the member movements of NSCF and its major program commissions (the Commission on World Mission and the Committee for Christian Work Among International Students) helped the Constitutional Revision Committee do its work in time to report to the NSCF Central Committee in February and again in April. By May 1, 1966—four months before the opening of the Eighth General Assembly—the proposed "amendment" was sent to all member movements, commissions, and sponsoring church bodies for their discussion and action.

Early in the summer of 1966, the NSCF received word that the Campus Commission of the Standing Conference of Orthodox Bishops in the Americas had decided to request full membership in the proposed University Christian Movement. And in August, the General Secretary of the NSCF was invited to attend the annual meetings of the national councils of the National Federation of Catholic College Students and the National Newman Student Federation, both of which were planning to consider a recommendation that they seek affiliation with the UCM.

It is impossible to describe the emotionally charged, searching, responsible debate which preceded the vote on the proposed Articles of Operation at the NSCF Eighth General Assembly. The final vote was unanimously in favor of the proposed Articles of Operation as amended during the two days of discussion.

The Preamble of the UCM Articles of Operation states, "We would emphasize that the organizational structure is not the movement, but exists to serve it." These words provide an important perspective from which to view this brief description of the machinery.

The Annual Assembly will be open to all who wish to attend, and "The primary function of the Assembly shall be to listen, to discuss and to reach to matters presented to it, to recommend priorities, policy and action in relation to these concerns." Also, "The General Committee will be a body of no more than 45 persons to be elected by the Annual Assembly, plus the officers of the UCM and chairmen of all standing and program committees. . . . The duties of the General Committee shall include making final decisions concerning policy, program, personnel and finances. . . ."

What the UCM does *not* propose to be is as important as what it does. At no point in the discussion of its formation has it been equated with the churches' total ministry within the academic community. As will be seen in the following quotation from the Articles of Operation, the UCM looks upon itself as a limited instrument with limited goals and abilities:

> The University Christian Movement has three basic purposes: (1) to serve as an ecumenical instrument through which members of academic communities can listen to, speak to and serve the Church and the University; (2) to encourage members of academic communities to respond to God's world in ways that will lead to fuller humanity for all men, to work for unity among those who are separated and to reflect theologically upon what they are doing; (3) to serve as an agency within which the church boards and agencies, the YMCAs and YWCAs and other sponsors of academic work around the world can serve members of academic communities by providing resources and offering opportunities for volunteer and professional service.

Who could predict what lies ahead for the University Christian Movement? It is still a frail infant which brings joy to many who behold it, but it has yet to prove whether it can prosper in an environment so full of problems.

The "generation problem" is never an easy one to solve. There will be misunderstandings and lack of trust between eager, impulsive students and more experienced, cautious elders in the churches and the universities. Those of us who are old enough to remember World War II are old enough to have become "evolutionists." Will we have the patience and understanding and trust which it takes to support our younger brethren in Christ who are deeply convinced that "revolution" is the only hope for mankind? Will we permit them the freedom to speak and act as if the Church, the university, and the state must be profoundly changed? Will we support their "radical" projects with the money which we, as part of the church power structure, control?

"Ecumenism" means different things to different people. Will those of us who believe it relates only to church institutions support the UCM, which openly confesses it is not a church, as it engages in what it calls ecumenical endeavors?

Many of us were trained to establish theological systems first and then to determine the proper behavior for Christians. Can we conscientiously support a University Christian Movement which believes that theological formulations must sometimes follow involvement rather than precede it?

The future of the UCM also depends in part upon its ability to decide what structural forms will aid "movement" and which will stifle it. Are denominational national student movements still needed? If so, for what purposes? What does it mean to be a responsible participant or member in a UCM which is as flexible and unstructured as this one?

We have no assurance that these and other serious problems will be solved satisfactorily. We do not know what unexpected joys and sorrows lie ahead for those who will serve within the University Christian Movement. But of this we can be certain: they will be challenged to faithful discipleship. What more can we ask?

III Ecumenical Openings Toward Contemporary Secularity

Like an eagle who rouses his nestlings,
Gliding down to his young,
So spread He His wings and took him,
Bore him along on His pinions.
The Lord alone did guide him,
No alien god at his side.

DEUTERONOMY 32:11-12

MOTHER ANGELITA MYERSCOUGH, Ad.PP.S.

5 Theology Courses in Catholic Colleges

To get into fruitful discussion on the topic of theology courses in Catholic colleges, I believe we need to think in terms of where we are and where we are trying to go, so as to assess the relative merits of how to get there. As an assist in this direction, I made a private, very minor sort of survey of the present practice of twenty Catholic institutions of higher learning which offer regular majors or fields of concentration in theology. Nine of these are universities; eleven are colleges. I believe they are a fairly typical sampling. Geographically, they are spread over fourteen states.

The objectives of the theology major program are not set forth in most instances. The five colleges or universities which attempt to state purposes mention one or more of the following as the goal or goals aimed at:

1. The opportunity to investigate the great body of Christian truth.
2. The opportunity for a student to gain understanding of Christian revelation, so that he may live a more profoundly Christian life in today's world.
3. The opportunity to study theology in order to prepare for responsibility and lay leadership in the Church.
4. The preparation of teachers of religion at elementary and secondary levels.
5. The preparation for graduate study in theology.

The kinds of electives that are being offered, judging by this sampling, vary considerably. Twenty-five percent of the presently described programs are quite traditional, using the same general course titles and course content as in past decades; about 60 percent I would characterize as in a state of transition from pre-Vatican II to post-Vatican II orientation; 15 percent show evidence of a thorough rethinking and reorganizing of the type of courses offered, both in content and in terminology employed in course titles and descriptions.

To break this down a bit more and look at specific areas, we find that courses in Scripture appear among the electives available in all these schools. But not quite all have a good selection of at least some in-depth courses in both Testaments. Only 15 percent have biblical background or language courses.

In the area of what we have traditionally termed dogma, 65 percent are using the traditional terminology and course content, such as *Dogma I* and *II; God, One and Triune;* and *Redemptive Incarnation.* Some 30 percent have set up dogmatic courses that are clearly intended to reflect the conciliar emphases, in both content and terminology. About 15 percent have dogma courses that are historically oriented or have development of dogma courses.

About the same picture is evident in the subject of Christian witness and living that we used to categorize as moral theology.

In ecclesial history or history of thought or patristics, 35 percent have traditional, period-type courses; 30 percent offer specialized courses.

Courses in liturgy and catechetics have understandably increased as standard electives: 85 percent of the schools in the sampling have some form of liturgy courses. Only 45 percent, however, have any type of formal catechetical work.

The thrust of ecumenical concern is evident in the fact that as of the year 1966-1967, 70 percent of these schools are offering some theology elective that aims at an understanding of the religious thought and practice of other than the Roman Catholic faith. This includes general courses in ecumenism, courses in contemporary Protestantism (40 percent offer this), special courses in contemporary theologies other than Roman Catholic (10 percent), and courses in the history of religion, the problem of religion, or comparative religion (35 percent). Ten percent have some course on contemporary Jewish thought.

Courses that show an awareness of a need to search out the vital interrelationships of the arts, literature, and other fields with theology remain at a minimum. However, three schools (15 percent) offer a course on literature and theology, and two schools (10 percent) have a generalized course in the area of theology and culture.

There are other courses, too, which cut through all the traditional categories into which we have tended to divide theology: 30 percent of the schools have some course that aims at studying contemporary Catholic thinkers, and 25 percent offer a study of the contemporary religious situation. Thirty percent continue to have a course on the lay Christian's role in the Church.

All told, this is not a very clear picture, but I believe that it does indicate ferment. It seems also to demonstrate a good deal of grappling with paradoxical aspects of the problem of college theology majors, such as the need to assure a good scientific grounding; a pastoral interest in the students' practical Christian living; a concern for both organized synthesis and historical perspective; and a need for fidelity to revelation combined with an urgent and genuinely honest searching into religious truth. The composite picture certainly evidences the fact that college theology teachers are much exercised by the obvious need for relevance to today's students. Finally, it seems rather clear that the practical problem of a dearth of well-qualified faculty is probably the most serious limiting factor in offering theology majors at all or in developing rich programs of electives for such majors.

RICHARD E. SHERRELL

6 The Department of Higher Education of the National Council of Churches

In the Division of Christian Education of the National Council of the Churches of Christ in the U. S. A., there exists a Department of Higher Education. With my tongue close to my cheek, I would like to paraphrase a well-known prologue: in the beginning was the *Commission* on Higher Education, and the Commission was with its Director, and the Commission *was* its Director, and the Commission became a Department and dwells among us. Thus, over a period of a decade and a half, is a concern about higher education in the minds of a few persons transformed into a bureaucratic structure with all the paraphernalia of committees and chairmen and budgets and programs and staff appropriate, or at least customary, for such an agency.

Of course, I speak about the work of the Department of Higher Education only as an individual. That disclaimer used to be made to safeguard the differing views of constituent members of the Council —but as some of us become more acquainted with Roman Catholicism, we begin to make the disclaimer to identify ourselves with the situation of diversity we find in Catholic affairs. The more I learn about your life, the more monolithic Protestantism appears! Thus are old stereotypes broken.

In the interests of brevity, I will try to illustrate the work of the Department of Higher Education with two examples. At the risk of some confusion in your minds, the examples will have to stand pretty much side by side without much clear evidence of interrelationship. While I do not think we necessarily have a corner on the confusion market, we do have a fair-sized piece of the action. We try, however, to think of our own confusion really as evidence of a creatively diverse range of interests and concerns.

One of our committees has focused over the years on the study and teaching of theology. The obvious contexts in which this activity has taken on Protestant form traditionally have been the departments of religion in church-related and private colleges and universities and in the seminaries as postcollegiate institutions. But all that is changing, as you are well aware. The most energetic and in some ways the most exciting developments in the study and teaching of theology are taking place in publicly supported institutions of higher education. It was with a view to this development that our committees generated a Consultation on the Study of Religion in College and University and Its Implications for Church and Seminary, held in New York City in early 1967. The Consultation brought together primarily Protestants from colleges, universities, seminaries, and denominational boards and agencies of education, but it was helped greatly by the participation of a few Catholics like Father Walter Burghardt, S.J., of Woodstock College and Father Gerard Sloyan of Catholic University of America.

The conclusions of this consultation are not yet firm, nor are the next steps in the process of evaluating what is going on entirely clear to us. A conversation has been begun between the traditional defenders and promoters of theological study and those new interlopers into the field who find themselves in publicly supported institutions. This conversation is good and must proceed. What I can report to you, however, is some of the input data of the Consultation.

Professor Robert Michaelsen of the University of California at Santa Barbara calls what has been taking place in recent years a "quiet revolution." Departments and curricula in religion, including graduate level work, now leaven the lump of American higher education. The biblical metaphor may be too strong for the facts, but the facts are impressive. What seems to be dominant in the facts is a widespread interest among students in theological questions, broadly speaking. The names of eagerly heard and read current thinkers are familiar—Bishop James Pike, Professor Harvey Cox,

Professor Hans Küng, and others. After his formal retirement from Union Theological Seminary, the late Paul Tillich probably spoke to more students than any other man in academia.

Born with the fall of atomic bombs on Hiroshima and Nagasaki; bred on Little Rock, Montgomery, Birmingham, Selma, and Watts; stunned by the loss of innocence in the death of a President; subjected to accelerated schooling after the sputniks; and crowded for space at all levels of life, this generation of students seems to sense the possibility of getting close to something meaningful in religion and theology courses in a way unknown in recent generations. How do these students feel about their experience in course-work study of theology?

Professor Michaelsen sent out a sixteen-question instrument to students at his own institution in Santa Barbara and to students at the University of Iowa. These students have all taken courses in religious studies. A few conclusions drawn by Dr. Michaelsen are the following:

1. Institutional church commitment seems to lie somewhere between "moderately strong" and "casual."
2. Courses are taken more for reasons of "intellectual curiosity" than anything else.
3. Neither the campuses nor the courses are overrun with atheists. Regarding the death-of-God debate (in which there is considerable interest), one student remarked, "If God is dead, why can't I smell him?"
4. Courses increase student interest in religion and do not seem to affect religious affiliation adversely; if anything, affiliation is strengthened by course work.
5. Sex morality, Vietnam, and the use of drugs are high on the list of moral concerns related to religious studies.
6. Speculative and avant-garde theology is of greater interest than historical and dogmatic studies. Vatican II in relation to other religions and birth control is of considerable interest.
7. Finally, while not being themselves pillars of the religious community, these students "are prepared to take seriously the church's or the Christian's boldest efforts to address the human condition today."

I dare say not much of these student data sound really new. What is new to all of us, however, and must be taken seriously by all of us is that academic nourishment of these attitudes and interests is an increasingly "secular" fact of American higher education. We in the Department of Higher Education want to stay abreast of these developments if we can, and we are interested in your participation with us in thinking through their implications for seminary and church-related forms of theological education, as well as in responsible support of these developments in public higher education.

The second dimension of the life of the Department I want to say something about has to do with faculty persons as such. A few years ago, as some of you may know, there was an organization called the Faculty Christian Fellowship. A quarterly journal, *The Christian Scholar,* helped give the FCF visibility and identity by dealing with some of the faith-learning questions of concern to the FCF. Over the country there existed what were called discipline research groups among faculty, the main purpose of which was to foster the faith-learning dialogue. While the FCF as such no longer exists, many faculty groups still meet (mostly on smaller private and church-related college campuses), and there are regional groupings around the country which assemble annually for conferences. There is still life among faculty who are concerned with understanding their profession and its context within higher education in some sort of Christian terms, though earlier hopes for a guild of Christian scholars did not pan out.

In place of the now defunct Faculty Christian Fellowship we have a new Committee on Faculty Interests. The task of this committee, composed primarily of faculty people from around the country, is to identify issues of particular concern to faculty, to reflect upon them, and to suggest ways in which they can be meaningfully approached from Christian perspectives. Such an issue, for instance, is the relationship between Christianity and the university intellectual, or academic man. In a recent document which was written to help get at this issue, the writer says:

> Is there any significant and fundamental difference between Christian and secular intellectuality? Certainly, it must be noted that the adjectives *Christian* and *secular* are not necessarily antithetical, whatever else may be meant by intellectuality. Is intellectuality more than rationality? Are there emotional, evaluative, volitional components to it? Can it be understood in some kind of functional or qualitative terms? For example, is there something about [the]

> work of university faculty that demands intellectuality? Probably we would all say we know too many nonintellectual faculty colleagues to be very comfortable with an easy affirmative [answer] to this question. Presumably, an intellectual is one who is critically aware of the presuppositions of his own work as well as being appreciatively aware of other ranges of thought and work. In what ways would Christian commitment qualify this awareness? Does all intellectuality imply a world view? Certainly, Christian intellectuality would imply such, but must this be true for all intellectuals, thus making a kind of comparison point? It seems reasonable that one identifying himself as a Christian intellectual should be able to say wherein his Christianity qualifies his intellectuality.[1]

The Committee has worked on these questions.

Another way in which the Committee on Faculty Interests co-operates with other patterns of life is through the publication of papers given at various conferences. In the Middle West there is an ongoing group called the Central States Faculty Colloquium. In the fall of 1966 it sponsored a two-day invitational conference at the University of Illinois. Four papers were read and discussed in depth. These have been published jointly by the Methodist Division of Higher Education and my office under the title *The Teacher in the University*. While the papers do not presume to cover all the issues involved in the subject, they do deal with cultural perspectives, objectivity, functioning *in loco parentis*, and student values as dimensions of faculty-teacher concern in the contemporary university scene. The publication can be had for the asking from my office.

Of course, the concerns of the Department of Higher Education are not limited to theological study and faculty interests. Space does not allow me to comment on campus ministry, on two of our "related movements" known as the Council of Protestant Colleges and Universities and the University Christian Movement, on efforts to upgrade predominantly Negro education, on the whole question of publication and mass media, or on a lot of other concerns that keep us at work, or at least off the streets (though it occurs to me that there is perhaps the most relevant place to be these days). We both respond to and take initiative on behalf of the churches for which we are an ecumenical agency. The problem

[1] Unpublished working paper.

is to find new and fresh ways of relating the resources of the Christian faith to issues in higher education. Sometimes the bureaucratic nature of the National Council of Churches is helpful in this effort, and sometimes it is merely frustrating. But a new day has dawned—there is new openness on our part and on yours. The issues are there. I am hopeful that we will discover new ways of getting over and around old barriers to find each other and join in the common tasks of the life of the mind and the life of faith.

SISTER MARY PIERCE BUTLER, M.S.B.T.

7 The Relevance of Biblical Language to Theology

What is the relevance of biblical language to theology? From one point of view, the question itself is surprising. It will be recalled that the intrusion not of biblical but of *non*biblical language was the problem faced by the early Church. The vocabulary forged by patristic theologians to express true doctrine and confound heresy—*homooúsios*, *hypóstasis*, and so on—while indispensable, remained somewhat suspect. Once the biblical faith was translated into other terms, there was always the danger of understating or overstating or misinterpreting the pure gospel. This distrust of an alien vocabulary, that is, of a technical theological vocabulary, is still alive in certain sectors of Christianity, for example in the antiphilosophical theologizing of many Protestants and Eastern Orthodox. But it died long ago in conventional Catholic theology.

We begin to see the dimensions of our problem when we consider that it is defined for us today as "What is the relevance of biblical language to theology?" and not "How can biblical faith admit of expression in nonbiblical terms?" Until quite recently, Catholic theology had grown comfortable with its own vocabulary, with its precise concepts and distinctions. It seemed to be satisfied—apart from the inevitable intramural debates—that the process of "translation" into neat formulas and propositions had been adequately carried out; and it was relatively indifferent to biblical scholarship.

With the Catholic biblical renewal, however, the picture changed remarkably. The return to the Scriptures brought new vigor into theological study, raised new questions, posed new problems. Scholars have devoted themselves to producing "biblical theologies" of seemingly every possible point of doctrine and facet of experience related to the biblical message. But it has not always been easy to see how the newly discovered (or rediscovered) expressions of the message can be integrated into the structures of systematic theology, or, for that matter, how they are to be related to defined dogma. The resulting tension, as it is described, for example, in Herbert Vorgrimler's collection *Dogmatic vs. Biblical Theology*, has given rise to fresh attempts to define the function and relationship of these two approaches to the gospel. The need to re-establish ties between biblical and systematic theology is all too evident to us and to our students. It is within this context, then, that our question is put.

Much attention has been drawn to the rich, concrete, personalistic character of biblical language as opposed to the terse, abstract, conceptualizing mode of speech used in the discourse of systematic theology. No doubt the nature of the theological enterprise demands a highly technical vocabulary; nevertheless, it is hard to maintain that nothing is lost when the lived experience of God's action in history is transposed from the language of event and encounter to the precise categories of theology. The ups and downs of the covenant relationship freely established by Yahweh with his Chosen People, for example, are minimized under the aspect of divine Providence, and the picture the gospels present of the man Jesus in the anguish of the human condition tends to be emasculated in dogmatic considerations of person and nature. The vivid imagery used by the sacred authors to describe the happiness of heaven is drained of almost all its color when presented as the "beatific vision," and abiding in Jesus as branches on the true vine is reduced to an impersonal level when thought of as "the state of grace."

In short, the systematic treatment of biblical faith cannot do full justice to its historically conditioned, incarnational aspects; it cannot represent in its proper categories the interpersonal dialogue between the "God who acts" and his people, or the dynamics of Jesus' personal life, or the many dimensions of Hebraic images.

The return to the sources and consequent recovery of biblical language has, as we have said, raised anew the translation problem—a question not to be answered by a simple linguistic key. Some discrepancy between biblical and theological categories is inevitable in the nature of the case. The gap has widened immeasurably in modern times, however, because men are not at home with biblical language to begin with. It has been argued, therefore, that the place to start the translation process is with the question "What is the relevance of biblical language to *modern man?*" We shall adopt this starting point, at least provisionally.

It would be naive indeed to address ourselves to this topic without consulting the course of discussions in the preponderantly German school of neo-Reformation or dialectical biblical theology. We must, of course, keep in mind the presuppositions with which these scholars approach the Bible. They would repudiate all that in their opinion interferes with the hermeneutical process by introducing a kind of false objectivity; therefore, biblical orthodoxy, authoritarian creedalism, positivist historicism, and metaphysical rationalism must all be set aside when the interpreter confronts the text.

In the view of the best-known representative of this school of thought, Rudolf Bultmann, biblical interpretation is the work of scientific and nondogmatic criticism which yet demands the "eyes of faith" if it is to yield understanding. Quite simply, Bultmann is concerned about the relevance of biblical language to our contemporaries, not to systematic or dogmatic theology. Because he takes language to be an objectification inappropriate to the subject matter—even a hindrance to understanding—he has in fact dispensed with the objectification necessarily involved in any intermediary systemization of the content of the Bible. Rather, Bultmann has identified theology with hermeneutic, a term now used to refer to the whole process of stating the meaning of the Word of God for our day (not, as formerly, in the sense of a theory of rules of interpretation). What, then, is the relevance of biblical language for modern man from this point of view?

We are all aware of the gap that exists between the mythopoetic language of the Bible and the language of modern man. Insofar as biblical language reflects a world view incompatible with contemporary science, insofar as it speaks of events which are incomprehensible in a twentieth-century frame of reference, it is a stumbling block, claims Bultmann. There is no need to burden the modern Christian with this unnecessary baggage; it is possible to strip the message of its outmoded oriental dress (which in any case is a linguistic objectification of an inadequate mythological conceptualization) and get at the core of its meaning. In other words, it is possible to arrive at the understanding which is prior to and more authentic than the language.

We are familiar with Bultmann's use of the Heideggerian analysis of the structures of human existence. This provides him with categories so universal as to be meaningful to men of all ages and all cultures. If the timebound statements of the Bible are reinterpreted in terms of every man's experience of existence, of fallenness and authenticity, they become grippingly relevant. Of course, Bultmann has embarked on a program more radical than that of an existential interpretation of the New Testament. His demythologizing seems to imply a thorough indifference to the factual and historical content of what is interpreted. This skepticism with respect to the objective reference of the gospel narratives rightly disturbs Christian theologians. To many, it appears that Bultmann is content to reduce the biblical message to one more philosophy of human existence. In Dr. John Macquarrie's helpful example, some feel that Bultmann regards the gospel record as a kind of ladder by means of which one is brought to the understanding of religious truth; once this self-understanding has been achieved, the ladder may be kicked away, for it has served its purpose. The devaluation of the historical uniqueness of God's revelation in Christ suggested by such a program is plainly at odds with Christian orthodoxy.

Macquarrie, in his book *The Scope of Demythologizing*, argues (very convincingly, I think) that Bultmann does *not* go so far as to kick the ladder away. He maintains it, writes Macquarrie, by insisting on the *kerygma*—the word of God to man proclaimed in his saving act in Jesus Christ. The purpose of Bultmann's demythologizing is to set the *kerygma* free, to liberate it from those antiquated expressions which modern man finds unacceptable. Christianity is not just one more statement of the possibility of existence, for it is rooted in an act of God in Jesus' life which gives man that possibility. As Macquarrie points out, Bultmann's conservative critics fault him with losing touch with this historical deed, while his liberal critics attack him for retaining it, for setting a limit to demythologizing. There is definitely a problem in showing how Bultmann holds together the two sides of his theology, demythologizing and *kerygma*.

Actually, this problem is very much the consequence of Bultmann's understanding of biblical language, and that is our reason for bringing it up. In his opinion, the appropriate language of religion is myth. "Mythology," he wrote, "is the use of imagery to express the other-worldly in terms of this world and the divine in terms of human life, the other side in terms of this side." [1] The meaning of myth for modern man lies in the understanding of human existence it expresses and not in the apparent objectivity of what is said. In practice, Bultmann regards as myth everything from the three-decker universe and the imagery of Jewish apocalyptic through miraculous cures and the spirit world to the virgin birth, the Incarnation, and the Resurrection. It appears that only the man Jesus and his cross are exempted from this category. How, then, is it possible to avoid the radical demythologizing that would undermine completely the reference to historical, objective fact? What saves Bultmann from going all the way?

According to Macquarrie, Bultmann rescues a minimal core of historical factuality when he speaks of the *kerygma* as "an act of God." This phrase, if it has any meaning, is analogical; that is, it has reference beyond human understanding, reference to the transcendent God. If Bultmann takes this seriously, he must admit at least implicitly a distinction between myth, in which symbol and symbolized have not been sorted out, and analogy, in which the speaker consciously employs symbolism.

This distinction to which Macquarrie calls attention in order to vindicate the paradox in Bultmann's thought may be found also in the theology of Paul Tillich. Tillich would agree that the language of faith is myth. Modern man, he concedes, is conscious of its mythical character. We can say, therefore, that he has "broken" the myth. Tillich calls the "broken myth" a symbol. Modern man retains symbols as the language of faith, though he is critical of their purported relation to time and space, because he has no other means of expressing the truth they embody. Tillich is frankly radical in his demythologizing; he extends it to both natural and historical myths, and effectively strips biblical religion of its content. Christianity is only a broken myth in which men have tried to state their "ultimate concern."

[1] Rudolf Bultmann, *Kerygma and Myth*, ed. Hans Werner Bartsch, New York, Harper & Row, Publishers, Harper Torchbook, 1961, p. 10, n. 2.

Let us take an example of the difference between myth and analogy (or myth and symbol). One who affirms "God is in heaven" may entertain a primitive world view which affords him no embarrassment in making this statement. Someone else may say the same without any mental picture of a spatial residence; "God is transcendent" is what he means by this. The former has a mythological, the latter an analogical (symbolic) frame of reference.

But let us pursue this a little further. It is quite gratuitous to suppose that the biblical authors lived in a world of unbroken myth, that what they affirmed could have been said in a plain, straightforward manner, had some modern only disabused them of their primitive cosmological views. It is indeed oversimplifying the issue to embark on a program of demythologizing which would extract the "content" from its symbolic dress and outfit it with a completely intelligible form. What lies behind this seems to be the assumption that scientific language is the model against which all serious speech must be measured. But is it fair to judge religious language by this norm?

In the words of Ian T. Ramsey, religious language is "appropriately odd." It deals with realities beyond the vocabulary of science and beyond empirical investigation and verification. Religious language is analogical and necessarily so. It is clear that to speak of God at all we must use terms from human experience. (This, you recall, is Bultmann's definition of myth.) We have no alternative. Whatever we affirm of God is going to be partial and imperfect and groping.

This would be true quite apart from the Incarnation; it is simply the nature of the case. But God has acted in human history, taken human flesh, spoken human words. And the men who have told us of this have communicated in human speech and in the images of their own culture. Jesus himself spoke in images and parables: the kingdom, the wedding banquet, his coming on the clouds of heaven.

What I am trying to suggest by these remarks is that the very legitimate attempt to translate biblical language for modern man is severely handicapped by the idea that myth is the language of religion. Even in Bultmann's very general sense of imagery which expresses the divine in terms of human life, or even from the point of view that all speech about God must be analogical and symbolic, the category of myth remains inadequate for biblical religion. It is inadequate, first, because it has no need of a factual, historical basis, and second, because it has no need of faith. Bultmann, we have said, is hard put to explain how he has not demythologized history and reduced biblical religion to an existential philosophy. But for his insistence on the *kerygma*, it would seem that the new self-understanding toward which mythology leads was available independently of God's saving act in Christ and of God's forgiving grace.

Tillich appears to have abandoned even these links with Christianity. The revelation of God in Christ loses its unique importance when, in the interests of ontology, one considers the framework of space and time alien to the nature of the ultimate. If, as Tillich would have it, faith is only "the acceptance of symbols that express our ultimate concern in terms of divine actions," [2] it is hard to see how religion is any more than a propaedeutic to ontology. The broken myths of biblical religion seem no more important than the symbols which any world religion might provide for the expression of universal and timeless truths.

In brief, these attempts at translating biblical language run the obvious risk of devaluating the Incarnation and its consequences. The scandal of God's involvement in human history is somehow lost in the effort to demonstrate the relevance of Christianity. If we are unwilling to follow this road of radical demythologizing, yet feel acutely the need to redeem the Bible from fundamentalist interpretations, where shall we turn? How is responsible demythologizing carried on?

So far, we have followed Bultmann's lead in posing the question as "What is the relevance of biblical language to modern man?" He attempts to bridge the gap between these two terms without any intermediary objectification or systemization. A student of his now making his presence felt in Europe, Heinrich Ott, has suggested that the whole question needs to be lifted out of the hermeneutical circle which includes only the believer and the text. If the translation problem is dealt with in a circle or arch that includes systematic theology, the task of understanding the subject matter that comes to expression in individual biblical texts will not be

[2] Paul Tillich, *Dynamics of Faith,* New York, Harper & Row, Publishers, Harper Torchbook, 1958, p. 48.

left entirely to the believer. Interpretation of the text requires, he insists, some view of the whole content of the Bible; when this step is bypassed, biblical language either remains meaningless or is open to misunderstanding.

Evident as this suggestion may seem, it provides, I think, some help in clarifying the question at hand. Let us spell out briefly what this larger hermeneutical circle implies. First, the exegete is responsible for examining the text as such. With the tools of critical scholarship he must demythologize the language of the Bible and attempt to determine what is revealed content and what is literary form (in the manner that scholars have interpreted Genesis 1-11). Then the theologian must take up all of the biblical revelation and look at it as a unity, relating part to part systematically and thus providing a framework for interpretation. Only on the basis of this understanding of the subject matter as a whole can biblical revelation be passed on to modern man in the Church's preaching. In other words, systematic theology has the role of mediator between the text and the believer, between biblical language and modern man. The faith which encompasses this circle precludes the demythologizing of history and the demythologizing of the *kerygma* as a gift of God.

In a way, this proves more about the relevance of theology to biblical language than vice versa, but since it is a question of a hermeneutical circle, the answer can be read both ways. Systematic theology stands in a relation of interaction with exegesis. If, on the one hand, biblical language needs the mediation of theology in order to be intelligible to modern man, on the other, systematic theology needs to be rooted in the language of history and experience of faith found in the Bible. Just as the radical demythologizing which cuts loose from history and faith by reducing biblical language to myth tends to bring forth an existential or ontological interpretation rather than Christian faith, so the systematic theology which refuses to take biblical language seriously threatens to betray the historical revelation it proposes to illuminate.

The relevance of biblical language to theology today, then, must be stated in terms of its role of grounding contemporary expressions of faith in the unique moment of history when the Word became flesh and in the experience of salvation which comes solely through the gracious act of God in Christ.

SISTER ALEXA SUELZER, S.P.

8 Theology of the Holy Spirit

Amid provocative and piquant concerns in current religious thinking, the topic of the theology of the Holy Spirit might seem curiously flat. And so it would be, I suppose, if we merely re-examined the sections of *De Deo trino* specifically devoted to the Holy Spirit. However, the intensity of the discussion over the Church and the modern world suggests a pertinent approach: the question of the mode of God's presence in this secular age. Hence, our purpose is not to re-examine or re-define but rather to speak of how the Spirit manifests Himself in our contemporary world.

Several factors dictate this treatment. First, Vatican II, in its spirit, in its working, and in its final documents, has underscored the charismatic, nonhierarchical elements in the action of the Spirit and has thus pointed up the barrenness and inadequacy of traditional pneumatology. Second, the growing involvement of the churches in the secular world points to the outpouring of God's Spirit beyond the confines of institutionalized Christianity, for there are many groups struggling for the coming of the Kingdom. Furthermore, certain radical theologians (notably Thomas J. J. Altizer and his school) employ a Hegelian Spirit-everywhere concept which must be noted in discussion with them and which must be dealt with in a modern theology of the Spirit.

Let us return to the first point, Vatican II's emphasis upon charismatic elements. The constitution *Lumen gentium* resulted from the conciliar efforts of the Church to reflect upon and define herself. Quite early in the debate it became clear that this definition could not be simply in terms of external institutional forms but must approach the Church as a mystery, that is, as a divine historical reality not to be captured fully by human thought or language. This desire to present the Church as a mystery leads at once to a theology of the Spirit, for the principle of this transcendent reality is the Holy Spirit—the Lord and Giver of life—operating not through the hierarchy alone but also through the entire people of God with their individual charisms.

But it is a sad fact that the Latin Church suffers from a very truncated pneumatic theology. In the West, ecclesiology has evolved in a juridical direction; in the East, the mystical, pneumatic aspect of the Church is much better developed. Both are essential. As the Eastern Council Fathers pointed out on many occasions, Latin ecclesiology is highly developed—even sophisticated—in the Christological dimension, but it is as yet adolescent in the dimension of the Spirit. Long centuries of overemphasis upon the hierarchical Church in the West have not only denigrated the charismatic elements but also subtly altered the position of the Holy Spirit: from the *life* of the Church, he became a static guarantee and sanction of ecclesiastical authority. The conciliar development of the concept of charisms among the people of God attempts to restore the balance; it is the greatest advance on this topic in centuries, and many years will pass before the consequences of this development will be adequately studied on the speculative level and implemented on the practical plane.

How does Vatican II speak of the Spirit's manifestation in today's world? In various ways, both within the Church and outside. In regard to the Church internally, *Lumen gentium* speaks of the Spirit working through hierarchical and charismatic gifts (though it might have more felicitously spoken of hierarchical and nonhierarchical charisms). The document does not treat charisms *ex professo,* but a working definition (based on Scripture and scholastic theology) can be derived from the conciliar thinking: charisms are perennial, necessary spiritual gifts granted by the Holy Spirit to *each* individual to enable him to fulfill his duties for the common good of the Church. To stress that all individuals enjoy such gifts, *Lumen gentium* specifies:

> He furnishes and directs her with various gifts, both hierarchical and charismatic, and adorns her with the fruits of His grace [sec. 4].

> Allotting His gifts "to everyone according as He will" (1 Cor. 12:11), He distributes special graces among the faithful of every rank. By these gifts He makes them fit and ready to undertake the various tasks or offices advantageous for the renewal and upbuilding of the Church, according to the words of the Apostle: "The manifestation of the Spirit is given to everyone for profit" (1 Cor. 12:7). These charismatic gifts, whether they be the most outstanding or the most simple and widely diffused, are to be received with thanksgiving and consolation, for they are exceedingly suitable and useful for the needs of the Church [sec. 12].
>
> On the contrary, they [pastors] understand that it is their noble duty so to shepherd the faithful and recognize their services and charismatic gifts that all according to their proper roles may co-operate in this common undertaking with one heart [sec. 30].[1]

From these passages, it is clear that the charisms here considered are the workings of the Spirit among the faithful. But what can be said of the Spirit's activity outside the pale of organized Christianity? This is a question which has scarcely been touched in Catholic theology; it is not surprising, therefore, that conciliar statements on the subject are a kind of *obiter dicta*, a point of departure, not a definitive summary. The fact of such manifestations of the Spirit is found in both *Lumen gentium* and *Gaudium et spes:*

> . . . many elements of sanctification and truth can be found outside of her visible structure [*Lumen gentium*, sec. 8].
>
> And there belong to it [the people of God] or are related to it in various ways, the Catholic faithful as well as all who believe in Christ, and indeed the whole of mankind [*Lumen gentium*, sec. 13].[2]
>
> All this holds true not only for Christians, but for all men of good will in whose hearts grace works in an unseen way. For, since Christ died for all men, and since the ultimate vocation of man is in fact one, and divine, we ought to believe that the Holy Spirit in a manner known only to God offers to every man the possibility of being associated with this paschal mystery [*Gaudium et spes*, sec. 22].
>
> . . . Christ is now at work in the hearts of men through the energy of His Spirit. He rouses not only a desire for the age to come, but, by that very fact, He animates, purifies, and strengthens those noble longings too by which the human family strives to

[1] "Dogmatic Constitution on the Church," in Walter M. Abbott, S.J., *The Documents of Vatican II*, New York, America Press, 1966, pp. 17, 30, 57.

[2] *Ibid.*, pp. 23, 32.

> make its life more human and to render the whole earth submissive to this goal [*Gaudium et spes*, sec. 38].
>
> She [the Church] also knows that man is constantly worked upon by God's Spirit, and hence can never be altogether indifferent to the problems of religion [*Gaudium et spes*, sec. 41].[3]

That the Spirit works in all men seems definitely conciliar teaching; *how* the Spirit works through non-Christian channels is a question the Council Fathers did not ask, much less answer. To divert emphasis from a Spirit-led hierarchy to a Spirit-led (charismatic) people of God (both hierarchy and laity) seemed accomplishment enough. The more delicate question of the manner of the Spirit's activity through other channels was not specifically broached. Eventually it will be treated: the seminal thinking of the Council Fathers will assure this, and so will contemporary Protestant theological speculation on the Spirit. The developed theology of the Holy Spirit will have to relate this activity to the more traditional (and more comfortable) treatment of the Spirit working within the Church.

Several other areas of necessary development suggest themselves. Increased concern with individual responsibility to the promptings of the Spirit will demand a reworking of ascetic theology so that asceticism will be a discipline more truly conducive to opening to the Spirit. Closely related is the topic of discernment of spirits in mystical theology; how, in the light of conciliar statements on charisms, can the voice of the Spirit be distinguished from the other voices clamoring for attention? Finally, it would seem that a developed theology of the Holy Spirit will provide the only means for reconciling freedom and authority, because such a theology will show us the Church as freedom precisely because she is obedience to the Spirit.

[3] "Pastoral Constitution on the Church in the Modern World," in *ibid.*, pp. 221-222, 236, 240.

ROSEMARY RUETHER

9 Two Types of Radical Theology

I would like to outline briefly two major typologies of death-of-God theology. I use the term *theology* deliberately, because death-of-God thought is definitely a point of view about the relation of God, the world, man, culture, and history. Hence, it is properly to be called a theology, however unfamiliar the concepts it uses may be to more traditional theology. Indeed, as I will point out, even in this area, death-of-God thought can be paralleled with other theologies, in that it is not traditionless but can be traced back through a considerable tradition in Christian theological history: in one case, through an orthodox tradition, and in another case, through a heterodox but nevertheless persistent tradition in Christian history.

The death-of-God theologies which I will use to illustrate these two typologies are those of Gabriel Vahanian and Thomas J. J. Altizer. I shall focus here on the way these two men use the term "death-of-God" as the central symbol of their theological work. Two others are often named as part of this school of thought: William Hamilton and Paul Van Buren. I will not consider either of them as adding to the present thesis. Hamilton is, to be sure, an explicit advocate of death-of-God thought, but from his writings no real theological rationale of this term can be discerned. In the case of Van Buren, although he is a theologian, he is not a death-of-God proponent but is really involved in a rather different project—the application of linguistic analysis to theological concepts. His view is that we cannot experience God directly but only as Jesus, the man for others. This is a perspective which could easily be assimilated into the Protestant Kantian tradition of the unknowability of the noumenal in itself, reality being known only through the phenomenal level. This point of view by no means need be equated with a programmatic use of the term "death of God" as a central symbol, and Van Buren has clearly expressed his desire to dissociate himself from the term.

This, then, leaves us with two contemporary thinkers who programmatically use the term "death of God" as their central way of expressing their theological position: Altizer and Vahanian. And, as we shall see, they use the phrase in very different ways.

Vahanian says "death of God" prophetically to break apart our sterile and empty cultural symbols of the divine. In doing so, he joins squarely in an orthodox Barthian and Calvinist usage. Vahanian's God is the biblical God who is radically transcendent of Creation and who is available only in revelation. The revelation of the "wholly other" is experienced as the shattering of human religiosity. For Vahanian there is no real question of atheism versus theism because man is an incontrovertibly religious animal. There is only the alternative of idolatry or iconoclasm. The biblical God is the iconoclastic God, the God who is imageless and who commands man to make no image of Him. He appears and is present to man in revelation in the mode of an idol-smasher, breaking apart our falsely infallibilized images and structures whereby we seek to capture the divine and put it at our permanent disposal. In this polemic against man's religiosity as incorrigibly idolatrous, Vahanian stands solidly within a tradition which goes back to Calvin and, behind him, through a Pauline-Augustinian strain in Christian thought. Vahanian himself, of course, identifies with the Reformed theological tradition.

Vahanian writes primarily as a theologian of culture, and he speaks of the death of God as a cultural phenomenon. The death of God expresses the ambiguity of man's cultural creations in general. Man stands between the poles of Incarnation and eschatology, between immanence and transcendence. The biblical God remains always transcendent, always the "wholly other." However, this does not mean for Vahanian that God is far away and inaccessible. Transcendency is not to be equated with absence; rather, the opposite is true. It is only as the radically transcendent one, as the "wholly other," that he can really be for us and save us. God's otherness and God's presence are not alternatives or opposites but rather univocal terms.

Only by remaining radically transcendent is God a "presence." He is wholly available for his creation not as one who fuses with his creation and becomes his creation but as one for whom creation is his self-disclosure and the arena of his glory. Creation is never confused with God, but creation is the arena of God's *shekinah*—God's presence, or what we would call "the Holy Spirit." We experience God's Word, God's presence, through the audible word, through the visible image, through the created work, but not as the created word and work. The created word and work must constantly negate or surrender themselves in order to be a place of disclosure of God's presence. This is the iconoclastic function of biblical religion—that is to say, the constant breaking apart of the creaturely desire to be *sicut Deus* in order that man may again be restored as the *imago Dei*. God's creation is God's image, but it is God's icon only in the modality of iconoclasm, whereas the fall of creation takes place in its desire to ontologize this revelatory function as a "nature" which it possesses in its own right.

The paradox of the serpent's temptation of Adam and Eve lies in the double meaning of the promise that, if they ate the forbidden fruit of the tree of the knowledge of *tob* and *ra*, they would not perish but would be *like God*. The serpent's lie is at the same time a distorted witness to the truth, as though the serpent can only lie by telling the truth in a malicious way. For man to be like God is at the same time to die, to lose his authentic creational relation to God.

In seeking to be *sicut Deus*, man ceases to be the *imago Dei*, and creation falls, ceasing to be a place of the disclosure of God's presence. In seeking to be grounded on his own act, as is God, rather than on the act of one transcendent to him, man exists in a way which is radically inauthentic for him. He falls into self-enclosure, and his works become idolatrous, mediating no longer a saving presence of God but only a demonic self-image which bears him along for a while but gradually reveals its emptiness.

In his analysis of theological anthropology, Vahanian reveals his fundamental continuity with the Barthian position which is common in neo-Reformation dialectical theology. It is this anthropology which underlies Vahanian's theological evaluation of the contemporary post-Christian cultural situation. For him, Christian religiosity is the root of the death of God, the basis of the post-Christian era. Christian man himself is the father of the post-Christian unbeliever, and this reflects the ambiguity inherent in the acculturation and institutionalization of biblical religion. The presence of God as an eschatological event cannot be objectified and taken into man's possession, but remains available to man to the extent that he does not try to finalize his own cultural expressions of it. In this way human culture is a constant improvisation upon the theme of God's presence.

Man must experience his encounter with God by dancing it out, celebrating it, expressing it in his cultural and intellectual works, but he has a persistent tendency to turn the Word of God which he seeks to express from a *mandatum* into a *datum*. He now has the Word of God as an infallible book or set of teachings, and ceases to be available for a new hearing of God's Word; God's Word has now become his possession and the source of authority for what has already "become." This transition, from freedom for the Word to objectification and finalizing of the Word, at the same time erodes man's sacramental power from his cultural images. His cultural expressions cease to mediate a living vision and become dead symbols which exploit the name of God for their own social perpetuation. Claiming the authority of the absolute, these finite structures grow authoritarian, founding themselves on the name of the Holy Spirit while the Spirit's truth becomes increasingly absent from them. Thus, the religious system grows sterile, and more and more people in the culture revolt from its tutelage, preferring to carry the name of atheist rather than bow to the god of the religious system. In this they are already closer to biblical faith than the religious man, but the religious man so calls the tune for faith, has so indelibly imprinted his face upon the cultural image of God, that man in revolt seldom succeeds in stripping off the mask. He doesn't overturn the system and recover a living God, but still operates within the logic of the system, though now by way of reaction. Hence does religious man produce atheistic man.

Here, for Vahanian, is the process which has generated our present post-Christian culture within the heartland of Christendom. Christianity lives on as a fossilized sect within the very world which it created, as a sclerotic condition deriving from Christendom's cultural annexation of the being of God. Vahanian calls this the death of God, the foundational cultural event of the post-Christian era.

When we turn from Vahanian to Altizer, we find virtually the opposite way of using the term "death of God." Vahanian is working within a traditional anthropology. Altizer, on the other hand, employs it to express what has traditionally been considered a heretical anthropology. By *heretical* I mean a mode of interpreting man's relation to the divine which has passed from Marcion and the Montanists to the left-wing Brethren of the Free Spirit in the Middle Ages, the seventeenth-century Ranters, and such thinkers as Nietzsche and Blake in the more recent period, and which the Church has always regarded with a sort of horror as a "diabolic" reversal of the gospel. Although there is not time in this brief discussion to trace the complex affinities of Altizer's thought to this tradition, it should be pointed out that Altizer's theological structure belongs fundamentally to this left-wing tradition, a derivation which does not seem to have been clearly recognized in the discussion of Altizer so far. The fact that this style of thought appears again and again on the left frontier of the Christian community and frequently produces a community of the "Free Spirit" devoted to living out its implications is a phenomenon which needs further examination. This is not simply in the sense of pointing out the "sinful propensities of man" but in the sense of examining the roots of Christian faith in a Pentecostal expectation which remains always frustrated in the historical church and finds outlet in the left-wing community.

In Altizer's *Gospel of Christian Atheism*, the term "death of God" expresses very much a revolt against divine transcendence. In the style of Nietzsche and Marx, God's transcendence and the image of the Father God, which expresses a divine mandate and which stands over against and judges man, are the enemy of man's life. God the Father comes into existence through an alienating projection of man's superego upon the heavens. In the process, man loses his own freedom and autonomy and subjects himself to a humiliating subservience to his own self-projection. The wrathful God of judgment is the expression of man's self-hatred and self-alienation. The Father God must die, must be killed by man, so that man can recover his autonomy and dignity; one might say his "immanent divinity."

The death of the Father is symbolized for Altizer by the incarnation of Jesus. God the Father is man's self-alienation and must be killed so that the human God in Jesus may be born. Altizer, then, has no use for the archetypes of creation or resurrection; these he sees as the subservience of the human to the transcendent which must be overcome. Theologically the only positive symbol for him is the Incarnation (fused with the Crucifixion), which he interprets as the voluntary self-immolation of the Father. Incarnation is the voluntary and salvific self-abnegation and kenosis of the Father by which alienating transcendence is overcome. Thus Divine comes to birth in human form, or again we might say, the human recovers its immanent divinity which it lost through its creation of the Father.

When we compare this point of view with Vahanian's, we should see that they are theological opposites. No doubt about that fact is possible now that Vahanian himself has published a new book, *No Other God*, in which he repudiates Altizer's intepretation of the term "death of God," labeling it as the ultimate expression of that idolatry against which his own theology contends. Vahanian speaks of Altizer's thought as the apotheosis of man's idolatrous religiosity, and says that Altizer has simply appropriated the death of God as a cultural event into a new metaphysics of self-deification instead of receiving it as a judgment against such religiosity. The contrast between the two becomes very stark. Where Vahanian wars against man's acculturated divine immanence in the name of God's transcendence, Altizer wars against God's transcendence in the name of man's immanent divinity. For Vahanian, it is man's cultural expressions of God which must die, be broken apart and deprived of their finality so that, in and through this judgment of the Spirit upon his dying cultural creations, man may again and again encounter the living God. For Altizer, this whole function of transcendence, otherness, and judgment threatens man's autonomy. It is nothing but man's own alienating self-projection, and the creating and judging Father is literally Satan. The creator God is opposed to the redeeming God, and Altizer, like Marcion, witnesses to the new incarnate God of love who is contrasted with the God of creation and of law.

Both Vahanian and Altizer are trying to say something about our present religious, cultural situation and the sterility of a past Christian culture from which we have become estranged. The problem with Altizer's interpretation of the meaning of this situation, however, is that the creator God can be killed only once within a particular world of thought, and, this done, we have a human immanence which has lost the power of self-transcendence and self-judgment. These functions depend on a God who must remain fundamentally eschatological.

Killing the principle of transcendence and judgment also kills the principle of renewal, and therefore is likely to bring to birth a totalitarian immanence which must be tyrannical, there being no longer any principle to stand over against it. This is in fact precisely what has always happened when an immanentist theology of radical incarnationalism takes over. We can trace the effect from medieval and Reformation radicalism and apocalyptic sectarianism on down to Marxist societies of our own time. The society informed by the death of the Father and the birth of an immanent kingdom in history is good only for the initial revolution which kills off the alienating forces of authority. But the new impetus itself promptly either turns libertine (in the sense of denying its further capacity for sin) or becomes authoritarian in a new totalitarian way.

I am not contending that this totalitarian state is Altizer's intention, any more than it was Marx's. Indeed, his whole theology, like Marx's social theory, is directed toward bringing in an era of perfect love and harmony. But it does appear that totalitarianism is the actual outcome of the application of a theology of the death of transcendence, because such an effort fails to take account of the conditions of historical existence under which the eschatological event must be experienced. It considers the incursion of the eschatological into history as itself a historical datum and fails to see that the eschatological event happens not *as* history but as the *end* of history. It is a power in history not because it translates itself into a historical fact which soon becomes a past fact but because it remains in the modality of the "coming God," who lies ever ahead of where we are and who can therefore ever break apart our inadequate representations of him and lead us to a renewed vision.

So it seems that a theology of the death of transcendence gives birth to a totalitarianism which has lost its openness to the future by wholly appropriating the future here and now. A theology of the relativity of human immanences, on the other hand, retains its freedom for a new future by rooting itself in divine transcendence, and this freedom for continued renewal is at the same time a freedom to let the old gods die.

IV Ethical Crises of Development in a Secular Age

You shall observe My laws and faithfully keep My norms, that you may live upon the land in security.

LEVITICUS 25:18

REV. DANIEL C. MAGUIRE

10 Modern War and Christian Conscience

Jesus had the enviable advantage of not being a professional ethician. He did, however, manage to render disquiet forever what might have been the peaceful science of ethical inquiry. He instilled into history a revolutionary moral impetus which, on contact, dissolves every limiting and comforting moral code. He rooted the mystery of love in the mystery of God and called us toward horizons of peace, fulfillment, and reconciliation so unreachable as to appear absurd. His vision remains to haunt us and to create a tension between our practicality and the hope that was in him.

We propose to study here the Christian experience in the area of war and peace. It is not in every way a pretty story, and those who would view our history as a continuum of triumph expanding toward the eschaton will find small comfort in it. But the study can be valuable, not only to illuminate our consciences in the face of modern war but as a typology of the various methodologies adopted by Christians going about the gritty ethical business of weaving the ideal into the generally unreceptive real.

There are few problems and possibilities that are not illustrated in the history of our encounter with war. We see there the games people play with Sacred Scripture, the Golden Age syndrome which idealizes our origins in a distorting glow; we see the contextualist's agonizing discovery that love dictates not only rules but also exceptions; we experience the need for a better theology of the magisterium in the area of morals and for a more nuanced conception of the *consensus fidelium.* First to Scripture, then to history, then to theological conclusions and prospects.

Scripture

The Bible gives generous opportunity to those who would theologize by toying with texts. The pacifist can read in Isaiah 2:4, ". . . they shall beat their swords into plowshares and their spears into pruning hooks." The crusader can reply from Joel 3:10, "Beat your plowshares into swords and your pruning hooks into spears. . . ." In Matthew 26:52, Jesus says, "Put your sword back into its place; for all who take the sword will perish by the sword." And Luke gives us the same Jesus saying, "And let him who has no sword sell his mantle and buy one" (Lk. 22:36). The Sermon on the Mount has the words, "But if any one strikes you on the right cheek turn to him the other also . . ." (Mt. 5:39). But when Jesus was struck during his trial, he did not turn the other cheek but rather protested (Jn. 18:22-24). And so on and so forth. But let us hope these games are finished.

For the men of the Old Testament, war was an inexorable fact of life. Yahweh was a Lord of hosts, and to him were ascribed Israel's victories. His wars, of course, were holy wars.[1] The prophets were often more sensitive theologians, but the theme of crusading war was never lost. It was often to prove a congenial memory in the history of Christianity.

In the New Testament, there is not the slightest evidence that pacifism or the eradication of war was a problem on which direct attention was focused. War, though virtually eliminated by the Pax Romana, was a known cultural reality from which Jesus felt free to draw parables (Lk. 14:31-33). Soldiering was not condemned. John the Baptist urged the soldiers to be content with their wages (Lk. 3:14). Jesus marveled at the faith of the centurion (Mt. 8:10). The Acts saw Cornelius the centurion as "a devout man who feared God" (Acts 10:2). The instruments of war appear in the Pauline literature to describe the struggles of the just man (Eph. 6:11, Heb. 11:32-34).

The New Testament is not, however, irrelevant to war. Its appreciation of the dignity of persons and the power of suffering love point to the genuine source of peace; in addressing the sinfulness

[1] Roland de Vaux, *Ancient Israel*, New York, McGraw-Hill Book Company, 1965, vol. I, Pt. III.

of man, it calls for surgery on the radical causes of war. The Sermon on the Mount gives the maximal goals for which we must hunger and thirst. It envisions the ideal life to be fully realized on the "new earth where justice dwells," but that ideal must even now give shape to our struggling liberty. The Christian must exist in creative tension, straining to incarnate the possibilities of the gospel.

History

How did the Christians handle the gospel of peace in a military world? It is consoling, in a perverse kind of way, to see that from the beginning they were divided on the solution to this basic moral problem. This division appears with the first evidence of Christians serving in the army. Some would serve and some would not.

The philosopher Celsus seemed to think that all Christians were pacifists. In criticism, he said that if all men were like the Christians, the king "would be left in utter solitude and desertion and the forces of the empire would fall into the hands of the wildest and most lawless barbarians." [2] Origen, responding to Celsus, supports this impression, saying that Christians do not fight under the emperor even if he should require it.[3] And Origen was a major influence in the East.

Other evidence, however, shows that Christians did serve in the army without scruple. Tertullian, who was personally against the whole idea, admitted in his *Apologeticus* around the year 197 that Christians could be found in palace, senate, forum, and army.[4] There is no sign of pacifism in the frontier provinces of the East, where immigration, barbarian style, made battle a necessity. The Thundering Legion of Marcus Aurelius, recruited in Armenia, had Christians in its ranks.[5] In Syria, the king of Edessa converted to Christianity without surrendering his military resources.[6] The lists of holy martyrs in East and West include the names of soldiers.[7]

[2] Quoted in Origen, *Contra Celsum,* VIII, 68-69.

[3] *Ibid.*, 73.

[4] Tertullian, *Apologeticus,* XXXVII.

[5] Roland H. Bainton, *Christian Attitudes Toward War and Peace,* Nashville, Abingdon Press, 1960, p. 68.

[6] *Ibid.*, p. 70.

[7] *Dictionnaire de Théologie catholique,* vol. VI, col. 1916.

The ambivalence of the situation is summed up in the story of a lad named Maximilian, who was summoned to military service and refused on the ground that he was a Christian and could "do no evil." The proconsul reminded him that other Christians saw no conflict here and many of them were in the army. Maximilian granted this but protested his own conscientious objection and was led away to execution.[8]

Pre-Constantinian Christian literature was not so ambivalent as actual practice. When Irenaeus wrote that Christians did not know how to fight and when struck offered the other cheek, he was speaking the language of Justin, Athenagoras, Tertullian, Cyprian, Origen, Minucius, and Arnobius. Some would like to see these men as the spokesmen of the golden age of pacifism. It seems, however, that this is a somewhat uncritical and romantic interpretation. These men spoke of peace where there was no war. Their pacifism was untested. The apologists among them were interested in showing that Christians were good, peaceful citizens and no threat to the empire. They did not have to accommodate their doctrine of peace to a context of war. Later, when such an accommodation was called for, few Christians demurred at bending their principles to the needs of new situations.

The legitimate conclusions from this period would seem to be these. (1) The early Christians brought from their encounter with Christ an unprecedented sensitivity to the horror of bloodshed, and they enunciated its basic incompatibility with the gospel ideal. (2) They did not hesitate to offer prophetic resistance to the power structures of the empire in matters of conscience. They did not retreat to a ghetto but, persecutions notwithstanding, became such a notable social force that the Emperor Decius was quoted as saying that he was less concerned over the news of the revolt of a rival emperor than by the election of a new bishop in Rome.[9] (3) Even when Christians were drawn into warring situations, they usually insisted that the ministers of the sacraments abstain, to maintain some minimal witness to the peacefulness of

[8] Thierry Ruinart, *Acta primorum martyrum . . .*, Ratisbon, 1859, pp. 341-342.

[9] In Hubert Jedin and John Dolan, eds., *Handbook of Church History*, New York, Herder and Herder, I, 380.

Christ. It was not much of a gesture, but in many instances in history it was all the Christians thought they could offer. It is difficult to say whether this preserved the creative eschatological tension or merely filed it away.

And then came Constantine. Christians had been remarkably strong in the persecutions. Only the convinced and the stout of heart were inclined to join their numbers. But even the strong grow weary; and when Constantine, with his reputation for religious tolerance, appeared among the contenders for the throne, Christian sympathies were with him. Soon their arms were with him, too. When he won his battle at the Milvian Bridge under the sign of Christ, he was accepted as God's anointed. Few historians would stake their reputations to witness Constantine's orthodoxy. His was a kind of political ecumenism which courted any divinity with potential influence. But for reasons too wrapped in myth to decipher, he won the empire under Christian auspices, and he gave full credit to Jesus. Eusebius records his prayer of victory: "Under your guidance I have begun and completed these salutary deeds. I had your sign carried before us and so led the army to glorious victories. . . . I love your name and honor your power. . . ." [10] The gentle Jesus had become a Lord of war! Jesus, by the way, did not confine his new military prowess to the West. A fourth-century bishop of Nisibis reports that in response to prayer, the Lord routed the Persians by sending a cloud of mosquitoes and gnats to tickle the trunks of the enemy's elephants and the nostrils of his horses.[11] This was admittedly hardly a match for the Milvian Bridge, but it does show some versatility.[12] Constantine's victory was a victory for the cross, and since neutrality of religions would be anachronistic in the fourth century, the followers of Christ had leapt from persecution to preferment. We are told that they "rejoiced about present benefits and looked forward to future ones," [13] and that "Bishops received imperial documents and honors and subsidies." [14]

[10] Quoted in *ibid.*, p. 425.
[11] Theodoret, *Historia Ecclesiastica*, II, 26.
[12] Jedin and Dolan, *op. cit.*, pp. 316-318, 426-432.
[13] Eusebius, *Historia Ecclesiastica*, 10, 9, 6–8; *De Vita Constantini*, 2, 19.
[14] *Ibid.*, 10, 2.

Theological Developments

Christian theology exulted no less than the people. Even before the victory, Rome and Christianity were seen as pitted together by providence against the barbarian and the pagan. Easily the fathers in East and West saw the new regime in eschatological terms.

But it seems that nothing does more to impede the eschaton than the illusion of its arrival. What really had happened was this: A crusading spirit had not as yet been born, but the sword had become a friend and was not about to be turned into a plowshare. Christians were glorying now not in infirmity but in power. The identification with the state had brought peace, a military peace, and an identification with military ends and means. Sensitivity about military service disappeared so completely that by the time of Theodosius II, only Christians were permitted to serve in the army.[15] There was a diminished sensitivity to bloodshed which would prove devastating in its consequences. Since a Christian is called to prophetic tension, nothing could befit him less than satisfaction with the status quo. But this precisely was the Constantinian mood. A new situation had brought a new morality.

The Just War Doctrine

Early Christian thinkers did not hesitate to borrow from the wisdom of pagan antiquity. They found there, among other things, a treatment of the justification of war. Traceable in its core to Plato's *Republic*, the theory of the just war sought to limit the inhumanity of war and to direct hostilities toward the restoration of a liberal peace.[16] Cicero in his *De officiis* enlarged the theory, stressing that war might only be conducted by the state with a discriminating view to the needs of postwar peace. Though Roman practice was not always up to the doctrine, the ideas did take hold. *Humanitas* was the ideal mark of a ruler, and the conquering Julius Caesar could break with harder traditions and build a temple to clemency.[17]

[15] *Theodosiani libri*, XVI, 10, 21, December 7, 416. See Bainton, *op. cit.*, p. 88.
[16] Plato, *Laws*, 628; *Republic*, 471.
[17] Bainton, *op. cit.*, p. 42.

Ambrose and Augustine, important magisterial figures, received this doctrine into the Church. The *De officiis* of Ambrose borrowed more than a title from Cicero. Ambrose shows us, too, the developing split in the Christian outlook. Addressing clerics, he could say, "The thoughts of warlike matters seem to be foreign to our office . . . nor is it our business to look to arms but rather to the forces of peace." [18] Then, with an eye on the barbarians, he wrote, "Not eagles and birds must lead the army but thy name and religion, O Jesus." [19]

Augustine seemed more aware of the discrepancy between word and sword, and brought a mournful mood to his analysis of war. The barbarians were pressing in Europe and Africa when he wrote, and war appeared as a sad necessity. He allowed war in self-defense, to rectify a failure, to make amends, and to obtain the right of passage through a territory.[20] Augustine was perceptive enough as a moralist to admit the legitimacy of compromise in a world where God is not yet all in all. He was perhaps less felicitous in two other moves that he made.

First, in order to ease the Christian warrior's pain at having to return evil for evil, Augustine, who would not allow a private citizen to kill even in self-defense, tends to blend the Old Testament idea of the God-inspired war with the idea that the power of the state comes from God. Thus a soldier preserves his innocence, even under a sacrilegious emperor like Julian, by the right order of obedience.[21] Surrender of personal responsibility to government and holy war are foreshadowed here.

Second, Augustine paints a picture of a warrior who goes to kill with love in his heart that is so unrealistic as to be macabre. "Love," he writes, "does not exclude wars of mercy waged by the good." [22] This presents the impossible but alluring vision of war as a conflict between the simply good and the simply bad. It is pure illusion (historian Roland Bainton mentions that a good

[18] Ambrose, *De officiis,* in Migne, *PL,* XVI; quoted in Bainton, *op. cit.,* p. 90.

[19] Ambrose, *De fide Christiana,* II, 16, in Migne, *PL,* XVI, 590.

[20] Augustine, *De libero arbitrio,* V, 12, in Migne, *PL,* XXXXII, 1227; and *Quaestionum Heptateuchum,* IV, 44, in *CSEL,* XXVIII, 2, p. 353.

[21] Augustine, *Contra Faustum,* in Migne, *PL,* XLII, 448-49.

[22] Augustine, *Epist.,* 138, ii, 14.

case might be made even for the barbarians[23]). But every warring man or nation tries to see it that way. And the very illusion is in fact a root cause of war.

The just war theory, having been formulated, quickly became irrelevant. From north and south and east the barbarians were coming, and the orderly peace of Rome was passing away. The barbarians' war was without nicety. To the civilization they overran, they were not only a military but a cultural and moral threat. A new creed, violence, was coming to compete with Christianity, and to show that there are various leavens struggling in the batch of society and that the Christian leaven does not always raise the dough. War was in the blood of these people. It held top place in their primitive religion. Their gods and saints and virtues related to battle. They took to Christianity lustily, but much of the "old man" survived the baptismal waters. Saint Michael replaced Wotan, their god of war, as the patron of battle. Saint Peter was lauded in their liturgy for flashing the sword against Malchus, without reference to the Lord's rebuke.[24] Some faintly pacific reserve finds its way into their hagiography, as in the story of Saint Gerald of Aurillac. This worthy man always fought with sword and spear turned backwards so as not to kill anyone. By a marvel of Providence, he always won. Saint Edmund presents a more genuine tension. He faced the Vikings alone and unarmed and was slaughtered, and appears as something of a Christ figure absorbing violence.[25] The barbarians' consecration of violence was thus not complete. It was unhappy destiny that the Church would complete it for them.

It is true that Church efforts were made to contain the tide. Up until the eleventh century, the penitentials continued to prescribe penance for soldiers who had killed in battle, however just the cause.[26] The participation of the clergy in war was never officially sanctioned. And the Truce of God was a colossal, if belated, attempt to educate men to peace. Starting in the tenth century at the initiative of local bishops, the truce banned all

[23] Bainton, *op. cit.*, pp. 99-100.
[24] *Ibid.*, p. 103.
[25] Stanley Windass, *Christianity Versus Violence*, London, Sheed & Ward, 1964, pp. 38-41.
[26] Bainton, *op. cit.*, p. 109.

fighting, under pain of excommunication, from Septuagesima to Pentecost, for all of Advent, and on all Fridays, Sundays, and holy days. Church properties and clergy were always exempt, as were peasants and pilgrims, agricultural animals and olive trees. From age twelve on, everyone was bound to take an oath to obey the truce and, ironically, to take up arms against those who would not conform.[27] One of these oaths comes down to us from the tenth century, in a form taken by a gentleman named Robert the Pious. Its wording tells much of the state of things.

> I will not burn houses or destroy them unless there is a knight inside. I will not root up vines. I will not attack noble ladies nor their maids nor widows or nuns unless it is their fault. From the beginning of Lent to the end of Easter I will not attack an unarmed Knight.[28]

Stanley Windass' remark comes to mind concerning the Truce of God: "The disease was too radical to respond to such first aid." [29]

If violence could not be banned or conquered, it could be diverted. This the Church did in the Crusades. It seems that the libido of violence is like the libido of lust, unconsciously in constant quest of an object. The object became the heathen, and the means the holy war. The rationalization was perfect: if the cause was God's, the war was blessed. What is new in the Crusades is that the Church instigates and sacralizes these wars. Battle against the infidel comes to achieve a sacramental importance. Pope Alexander II launched the first salvific war, sending troops to Spain to fight the heathen Saracens. A kind of plenary indulgence was granted to all who fought. The Spanish were not a little confused by the adventure; for them, it was an internal problem not at all viewed in Christian-versus-heathen terms. El Cid, the hero of the time, often fought with the Saracens when their interests would coincide.[30]

The formal start of the Crusades came with Blessed Urban II at the Council of Clermont in 1095. Fulfilling the expressed hopes of his predecessor, Pope Saint Gregory VII, Urban set the Cath-

[27] *Dictionnaire de théologie catholique,* vol. VI, col. 1920.
[28] Quoted in Bainton, *op. cit.*, p. 110.
[29] Windass, *op. cit.*, p. 43.
[30] Philip Hughes, *History of the Church,* New York, Sheed & Ward, 1952, II, 251.

olic world ablaze with crusading zeal. The purpose of the movement: to reunite Christendom and establish Jerusalem as the center of Christian holiness. The sword had been given a prime role in establishing the Kingdom of God. The hundreds of bishops and abbots and the thousands of laity in attendance roared their approval. A plenary indulgence was declared for all who died in battle.[31] The greatest public relations job in the history of the Church followed the Council as Pope and bishops and monks scurried about the continent preaching the Crusade. The confusing, hopeless slaughter had begun in the name of Jesus Christ.

Ideological wars tend to be the cruelest; the Crusades witness this. A cargo of noses and thumbs sliced from the Saracens was sent back to the Greek Emperor . . . gory witness of crusading zeal.[32] The following account of the capture of Jerusalem comes down to us:

> Some of our men (and this was more merciful) cut off the heads of their enemies; others tortured them longer by casting them into the flames. Piles of heads, hands, and feet were to be seen in the streets of the city.
>
> . . . in the temple and portico of Solomon, men rode in blood up to their knees and the bridle reins . . . this day, I say, marks the justification of all Christianity and the humiliation of paganism.[33]

The consecration of violence was formalized. The Knights Templar were founded and vowed to fight in poverty, chastity, and obedience—an unholy marriage of violence and monastic perfection.[34] A new way of perfection was heralded for knights and lay folk. A contemporary wrote, "They need not go into a monastery nor renounce the world by vows, but they can win God's grace in their laymen's clothes and in their accustomed freedom." [35] And their accustomed freedom was considerable. Swords were blessed with liturgy so that those who wielded them in piety

[31] Bernhard Poschmann, *Penance and the Anointing of the Sick,* New York, Herder and Herder, 1964, p. 218.

[32] Bainton, *op. cit.*, p. 112.

[33] *Historia Francorum* in *Parallel Source Problems in Medieval History,* Frederick Duncalf and August C. Krey, trs., New York, Harper & Brothers, 1912; quoted in Bainton, *op. cit.*, pp. 112-113.

[34] Hughes, *op. cit.*, II, 299, 300.

[35] Quoted in Erdmann, *Die Entstehung des Kreuzzugs-Gedankens,* Stuttgart, 1935, p. 311; in Windass, *op. cit.*, p. 50.

might crush their foes with vigor through Jesus Christ Our Lord. A new situation had yielded a new morality. Neither in the hierarchy nor in the faithful was effective protest to be found. The radical discontinuity was ignored.

Heresy, too, was fought with the sword as indulgenced warriors struck at the Cathari in southern France. When the papal legate was asked how to distinguish between the Cathari and the Catholics, his reply shocked no one: "Kill them all; God will know which are his." [36]

Gratian's decree, which was staple legal fare from 1140 to 1917, says that to die in combat against the infidel is to merit heaven.[37] Saint Thomas Aquinas shows that war posed no major problem for medieval thinkers. In a classical example of theology answering the wrong questions, he has only one question on war in his *Summa Theologiae* as opposed to twenty-four long ones on angels.[38]

In the theory of the just war and the spirit of the Crusades, we have the elements of subsequent Christian theory and practice. We naturally tend to see war as either a crime or a crusade, and so we see our foes as criminal and ourselves as God's avenging angels. This historically derived syndrome is still operative. The image of Christendom versus heathendom becomes righteousness versus evil.

This was the mind set of the mellifluous Bernard, urging the crusaders, and of Luther, exhorting the princes to battle.[39] This was the spirit of Zwingli, who died in battle against the Catholics, and of Calvin, who said that no consideration could be paid to humanity when the honor of God was at stake.[40]

While some Renaissance humanists were expressing prophetic horror at the picture of society caught in its own frenzy of violence, the neo-Scholastics, with marvelous detachment, systematized the concept of the just war as an instrument of justice. Suarez, with an eye on the wars with the heretical English, stressed the obedience of subjects to the sovereign state.[41] There were no rules

[36] Quoted in Bainton, *op. cit.*, p. 115.

[37] *Decretum Gratiani*, pars II, caus. XXIII, q. V, c. 46; pars II, q. VIII, c. 9.

[38] Thomas Aquinas, *Summa Theologiae*, IIa IIae, q. 40.

[39] *Weimarer Ausgabe*, I, 535.

[40] John Calvin, *Calvini opera*, in *Corpus reformatiorum*, VIII, 476; XXIV, 360; XLIV, 346.

[41] Francisco Suarez, *De bello*, sec. X of *De legibus ac Deo legislatore*.

for the other side since the theory presumes them wrong and there are no rules for being wrong. Francisco de Vitoria (or Victoria), from his library, justified the Spanish plundering of Central America with the just-war right to passage through a territory.[42] Meanwhile, the Indians of Peru felt that the cruel Conquistadores were not born of women but rather must have emerged from the roaring sea.

Pacifism appeared in various Christian groups, the Anabaptists, the Quakers, and the Franciscan Tertiaries. The Quakers represent the most effective and enlightened reaction. They resisted the Augustinian and Lutheran tendency to leave to the state the decision on the justice of a war, and won exemption from conscription on conscientious grounds from the English state in 1802. They thus brought the state to honor a conscience with which it did not agree.[43]

The great wars of the twentieth century gave opportunity for the crusade to appear in modern dress. The announced goal now was not to unite Christendom but "to make the world safe for democracy." Churchmen in every land joined with their governments as World War I broke out. The just war theory was working for both sides. When the war ended, Germany was saddled with immense reparations on the shortsighted presumption that she was solely responsible for the conflict. The image had to be maintained that this had been a war of mercy waged by the good.

The tragedy of errors flowed through the pacifistic 1920s, setting the stage for World War II. Simplistic Americans would like to think that a goodly people were attacked at Pearl Harbor and that chaste honor propelled them into war. Historians of this period have little comfort to offer such romanticism. This is not to say that war could have been entirely avoided; but like every war, it was generated in an insensitive confusion amid extensive popular apathy.[44]

[42] Franciscus de Victoria, *De Indis et De jure belli relectiones*, Classics of International Law, no. 7, ed. James Brown Scott, Washington, D. C., Carnegie Endowment for International Peace, 1917, pp. 163-187.

[43] Bainton, *op. cit.*, p. 161.

[44] *The Saturday Evening Post* of May 24, 1941, editorialized that we were committed to war and that only a repudiation of our government could stop the shooting. Japanese assets in the United States were frozen as of July, 1941, and trade restrictions were so effectively applied that *The New York Times*

Perennially, the just war doctrine urged what is called the principle of discrimination involving noncombatant immunity. As technology grows, discrimination diminishes. In 1939, President Roosevelt said, "The ruthless bombing from the air of civilians in unfortified centers of population has profoundly shocked the conscience of humanity." He urged that nations should "in no event undertake bombardment from the air of civilian populations." [45] But then came Coventry, Birmingham, Hamburg, Dresden, Hiroshima, and Nagasaki. By the time of the atomic bombings, the word *target* had come to include population centers. And there was virtually no protest from the churches! [46] (A cynic has suggested that if we had dropped contraceptives instead of bombs on those cities, Catholic indignation would have flared.) The day was ruled by the demand for unconditional surrender, a typically infantile need observable in any street fight. And when victory followed all of this, we brought the vanquished to trial for their crimes! And why not? A war of mercy had been waged by the good!

For the past twenty years, the problem of war has been largely linked with the Communist revolutions. The Christendom-versus-heathendom syndrome is perceptibly operative in this encounter with the crusader's need to see his side as simply good and the enemy's as simply bad. Such a mentality cannot yield a nuanced and flexible policy capable of responding to change. The mentality is fortunately being dissipated by recent developments within the Communist world, and by the realization in some quarters that in a few years we might be grateful for any government, however undemocratic, that can feed its people.

During this period, weaponry has changed qualitatively. Thermonuclear war, with effects so devastating as to beggar the imagination, is now possible. A balance of terror has ensued and produced "peace of a sort." [47] It has also thus far proved Paul Ramsey's

---

could report on December 2, 1941, "Japan has been cut off from about 75 percent of her normal imports as a result of the Allied blockade."

[45] Quoted in John C. Ford, "The Morality of Obliteration Bombing," *Theological Studies*, September, 1944, p. 262.

[46] See James W. Douglass, "Notes and Reviews: Peace and the Overkill Strategists," *Cross Currents*, Winter, 1964, pp. 101-103.

[47] "Pastoral Constitution on the Church in the Modern World," sec. 81, in Walter M. Abbott, S.J., ed., *The Documents of Vatican II*, New York, America Press, 1966, p. 294.

statement that modern war is not nuclear war. "Instead, the possibility of nuclear war has made the world safe for wars of insurgency." [48] At the heart of our mammoth new strength there is this weakness, as Mao Tse-tung, Ho Chi Minh, and Che Guevara have discerned.

So we find ourselves in Vietnam at war again, in a war which is ambiguously called "limited" since it is nuclear-free but which involves American prestige and anti-Communist ardor, neither of which bespeak a limit. The war is distinguished by the fact that no war has ever evoked such open dialogue between conscience and strategy. Awakening consciences are anxious for facts and resentful of "the credibility gap," a term which has appeared during the Johnson administration to describe a reality which is as old as war. Let us hope that some theological perspective on this situation is suggested by our history and our conclusions.

Conclusions

Our primary conclusion must be an act of sorrow. We should view our history from the Milvian Bridge to the Mekong Delta and admit that we have poorly served the God of peace and too glibly called ourselves Christians.

Our theological conclusions touch on three points: (1) the teaching role of the Church in morals, (2) the role of the individual Christian, and (3) the conversion from a theology of war to a theology of peace.

The Teaching Role of the Church

Our experience in this important area of morality might well prompt us to describe our competence in teaching morals in more modest language which will not be embarrassed by our history or offensive to morally perceptive good men outside the Church. Ideally, the voice of the moral magisterium would be prophetic, creative, and dialogic.

Prophetic: We are all imbibers of our environment, passive absorbers of the spirit of the day. The role of prophecy is to pierce the enveloping cloud. The Middle Ages were a time of violence;

[48] Paul Ramsey, "Can Counter-Insurgency War Be Conducted Justly?", paper delivered before the American Society of Christian Ethics, Evanston, Illinois, January 22, 1966.

in a violent age the Church acted violently. It was largely absorbed and did not break through. Pope John, in our day, spoke prophetically, and Paul Tillich called his work utopian—a charge every prophet is liable to, since he speaks a word for which the world is not ready. But speak it he must, so that it may begin to take on flesh. The institutional Church must be an institutional prophet, avoiding the conservative tendency of every institution to identify with the structures that support it.

Creative: Lack of ingenuity is a great sin in a teacher or a teaching Church. We must not eschew the science of public relations and group dynamics. If Christians are still insensitive to the horror of war, if they can rest while their brothers die, then a massive re-educational effort is needed. The Church must learn how to speak better. And it must speak less as a judge than as an imaginative and creative force in society.

Dialogic: The magisterium must never feel that it is detached from the society of men in order to pronounce *licet*s and *non licet*s upon the passing scene. It is part of the world and the dialogue thereof. The bishops' statement on war in the fall of 1966 gave a perfect example of the dialogic magisterium:

> We realize that citizens of all faiths and of differing political loyalties honestly differ among themselves over the moral issues involved in this tragic conflict. While we do not claim to be able to resolve these issues authoritatively, in the light of the facts as they are known to us, it is reasonable to argue. . . .[49]

This is a humble statement, sensitively in dialogue with the context, aware that morality involves not a bundle of truths to be dispensed but the delicate application of principles to changing facts. The bishops, in further honest witness to the delicacy of complex moral judgments, explicitly conceded to Catholics the right to conscientious objection to the position expressed.

Should it become necessary to change the views given in such a statement, it would not be an embarrassed retreat but a new phase in a continuing conversation.[50]

[49] *The Pastoral Statement of the Catholic Bishops on Peace in Vietnam*, Nov., 1966.

[50] Gregory Baum, O.S.A., "The Magisterium in a Changing Church," in *Concilium*, vol. XXI: *Man as Man and Believer*, Glen Rock, N. J., Paulist Press, 1966, pp. 67-83; see especially Yves Congar, O.P., *Chrétiens en dialogue*, Paris, 1964, p. 79.

It might be well to note, as we move to a belated refinement of the theology of the magisterium, that the magisterium teaching morals and the magisterium teaching dogma might usefully be distinguished, since they present different problems.[51]

The Role of the Individual Christian

The statement of our bishops on war said, "No one is free to evade his personal responsibility by leaving it entirely to others to make moral judgments." The bishops went on to urge each person's duty to seek alternatives to the present conflict. John Courtney Murray wrote in 1959, "War is not simply or even primarily a problem for the generals or the state department. . . . Here, if anywhere, 'The people shall judge.' . . . This duty in social morality is being badly neglected in America at the moment."[52] Never does the government stand more in need of Christian witness than when it has embarked on a national policy involving the destruction of life.

Let the individual Christian take these considerations to heart:

1. Do not blame the government for mistakes that have been made and are being made if you are content, like the lowing herd, to wind slowly and unknowingly o'er the lea. Do not accuse our bishops of ineffective leadership. History shows that people tend to get the leadership they deserve. When there is enough initiative from "below," leadership responds.

2. The terms *moral* and *political* are distinguishable but not separable. The medieval Church can be accused of meddling in state affairs, but at least it recognized that what involves men involves morality.[53] Its sin was less grave than the modern heresy which says that certain policies are political and strategic and therefore immune to moral criticism. The most recent form of this heresy

[51] Some of the special problems of the moral magisterium are attracting attention. See John J. Reed, S.J., "Natural Law, Theology, and the Church," *Theological Studies*, March, 1965, pp. 40-64; John L. McKenzie, S.J., "Natural Law in the New Testament," *Biblical Research*, 1964, pp. 1-11; Gregory Baum, O.S.A., "The Christian Adventure—Risk and Renewal," *Critic*, 1965, pp. 41-53.

[52] John Courtney Murray, "Remarks on the Moral Problems of War," *Theological Studies*, 1959, pp. 46-47.

[53] Alfonso Stickler, *Il Potere Coattivo Materiale della Chiesa nella Riforma Gregoriana secondo Anselmo Di Lucca*, Studi Gregoriani II, Rome, Abbazia Di San Paolo, 1947, pp. 235-285.

absurdly alleges that selective pacifism is political and not moral.[54]

3. Since you are morally responsible for what your government is doing, acquaint yourself with the facts. Our principle-inclined tradition has made us somewhat fact-shy. Ill-informed or uninformed protest is a disservice. The facts are available, and a free society is proving its ability to get to them.[55] Of course, you needn't have all the facts to enter the debate; such a requisite would preclude all human conversation. Truth is reached in process. Prentiss Pemberton reminds us, "Most of the peace aims now being affirmed by our government were declared first not by Washington but by critics of our policy." [56]

Protest does tell. Protest should not, however, take place under the banners "hawk" or "dove." The complexity of the present conflict does not admit of such artificial polarization. These terms rationalistically imply that you must unqualifiedly adopt position A or position B. In this area, as in any complexity, truth is served by a flexible interchange and constant adjustment. The pursuit of *an* answer is a quest for the mythical Holy Grail.

A Theology of Peace

No people ever thinks of itself as barbarous, although subsequent ages nearly always see it as such. Our too facile acceptance of war may seem incredible insensitivity in ages to come. War must be seen as a social problem to be done away with, not something to be justified by a contorted casuistry. It must be seen as it is—a deterioration of politics. Theology must address itself to the complete human problem and focus the light and hope of the gospel on all the miseries that breed hostility and contempt. Christians, institutionally and personally, must be among men as brothers and suffering servants, more energetically and more ingeniously witnessing the Lord who wept at man's insensitivity and inability to know the things that are for peace. We must dare to share his dream of oneness and love among men. We have no alternative.

[54] *The National Catholic Reporter* of March 15, 1967, gives the report on page 1 of the National Advisory Commission on Selective Service. According to this group, selective pacifism is "essentially a political question of support or non-support of a war and cannot be judged in terms of special moral imperatives."

[55] See the editorial comments, *Saturday Review*, March 25, 1967, pp. 22-23.

[56] Prentiss L. Pemberton, "U. S. Policy in Vietnam," *Cross Currents*, Spring, 1966, p. 136.

M. RICHARD SHAULL

11 Confronting the Power Structures: Cooperation or Conflict?

In order to provide some stimulus for discussion, I would like to state four points, briefly and sharply.

First, it is only fair to present explicitly the perspective from which I as a theologian attempt to work on problems of Christian social responsibility. My orientation is fundamentally eschatological in character: the *coming Kingdom of God* is the focus of our attention. This means that our vision of the type of society for which we struggle is not determined primarily by certain principles deduced from a metaphysical world view, nor by a theory of natural law, but rather by the biblical and theological descriptions of the shape of the new humanity—the picture of the new man within a transformed social order.

When this is our starting point, we get our bearings not so much from past achievements as from future "utopias," that is, from an ongoing reflection on the ways by which the concrete potential of the present can be transformed into actuality on the road to the future. In eschatological perspective, we not only believe that a new future is possible; we are convinced that this future is now taking shape in our midst. Therefore, we do not require a blueprint before us in order to move expectantly ahead. We are free to put the fragments of our knowledge together into some more or less coherent picture, as we reflect upon the concrete materials provided by sociological analysis in the light of the understanding of the human and of history provided by biblical and theological symbols. In other words, we are free to participate in the task of formulating and reformulating secular political ideologies.

In this context, the future becomes an explosive force in every present; the coming Kingdom of God stands in judgment over every status quo. Christian existence is revolutionary existence. It is participation in the work of Christ who "has made all things new" and invites us to share in this transformation of the world. As Professor Roger Mehl has said, the lordship of Christ "breaks the established order, the established injustice, and calls us to take part in the great renewal of history." [1]

Through eyes of faith, we perceive his spirit at work in our recent history, undercutting the authority of old structures, liberating men and women from the dominance of old ways so that they may move to new experiences and new awareness, and raising up messianic movements that call our attention to old injustices and point us toward new possibilities.

This does not mean, however, that every Christian should be a political revolutionary in all situations. In a society torn by chaos and confusion, he may see his mission as that of working for order and stability. In a situation in which institutions are oriented toward the future and provide a framework for effective changes in society, Christian concern will probably express itself mainly in working within the established structures according to the generally accepted rules of the game. But in circumstances where pressures for needed change are met by effective means of control, and where no political instruments exist by which major social transformation can occur, the Christian is free to be a revolutionary.

As my second point, I would defend the thesis that we in America now find ourselves in such a situation. We are slowly awakening to the fact that modern technology, as it now functions within the framework of our institutions, is gradually creating a system of domination which, if allowed to develop on its own, may reduce us to one-dimensional existence. And this is happening at the precise moment when the marginalized and dispossessed people of all classes, groups, and races around the world

[1] Roger Mehl, quoted in John Bennett, ed., *Christian Social Ethics in a Changing World,* Student Christian Movement Press, London, 1966, pp. 52-53.

are coming to a new awareness of their historical existence, and are calling for a new opportunity to live in freedom and assume some responsibility for the shaping of their own future. This intense longing of the internal and external proletariat of our modern world is being increasingly blocked by the system of self-preservation and control of which we are now a part.

The awareness of these new developments has not come primarily from the intellectual and spiritual leaders of our nation, but from a quite different source—the new leadership of the dispossessed, and the new generation. For most of them, this discovery has come as quite a shock. Negro and white young people in the civil rights movement began to march with very limited and specific objectives. Eventually, they discovered that, in the South, they were up against a whole structure of power, institutionalized in social, economic, and political organizations, and that this was not going to change readily. When the struggle shifted to the northern urban centers, the same problem became even more evident. And there a further complication appeared. As automation develops, several million people in our society simply have no place in the productive process because they do not have the skills called for. Efforts can be made to train them, but the problem has its roots in our present economic order; only if we can bring about certain fundamental changes in it can we meet the challenge before us.

In the same manner, young people who have gone to Asia, Africa, or Latin America with the Peace Corps or with other volunteer study and work programs have discovered that the problems in these nations are complicated by *our* system of economic, political, and military influence and domination. Our present relationship preserves a situation that is favorable to us and unfavorable to them; and our foreign policy seems more and more geared to maintaining the present structures at any cost. Some of these young people have gone from their experience in the Third World to the slums of Harlem, Watts, or Chicago. There they have become aware of a pattern of internal colonialism that is very similar to what they found abroad. The people in our urban ghettos are also subject to external political and economic forces over which they have no control, and they now have no way of doing anything effective to change their situation.

Universities and professional schools across the country are also scenes of great unrest. Those who are most sensitive to what is happening are convinced that our education system today is inadequate to our needs. But it is very difficult to get at the heart of the problem. Not only does the general structure of our education institutions direct the attention of students, faculty, and administrators away from it; what is much more serious is the fact that the system functions so effectively in dealing with isolated problems. Only in rare instances can these become occasions for more serious reflection and action in relation to the underlying issues.

This does not mean that we are victims of a conspiracy on the part of evil men. What I am arguing is that we are part of a system—together with an ethos which goes with it—that, *if allowed to continue in the direction it is now taking,* will become more and more dehumanizing. The system has almost unlimited possibilities for meeting the material needs of men, but as it now functions within present structures, it has excluded almost a quarter of our own population from these benefits. And it perpetuates a relationship between rich and poor nations which broadens the gap between our affluence and their poverty every year. The system provides people with extraordinary opportunities for awareness, experiences, and contacts; yet it does not offer them any real chance to participate in the major decisions affecting their lives.

We gradually become aware of the degree to which we are subject to a structure of domination, and the fact that this totalitarianism is bland rather than harsh does not make it any less dangerous in the long run. Moreover, the system is intent on its own preservation; all forms of protest and dissent are allowed as long as they do not threaten the basic structures. When groups in any society commit this unpardonable sin, they are denounced as "subversive," and can be controlled by the resources which advanced technology provides.

This brings me to a third point. Those who see the need for fundamental changes in the structures of our society and in the direction in which it is moving are convinced that such changes are practically impossible in the foreseeable future. The present system may not be able to satisfy our most basic human needs.

But it is very effective in satisfying partial and false needs of large segments of the population and thus of maintaining their loyalty. It offers great rewards to scholars and intellectuals, businessmen and politicians who play the game; and recent revelations regarding the work of the CIA show how effective it can be in neutralizing large numbers of our more progressive leaders. For a variety of reasons, most of us have no basis for making a radical critique of the system as a whole; conservatives *and* liberals now function in terms of the same basic presuppositions. By and large, in art and in music, in literature and philosophy, in the social sciences and religion, we have so restricted our universe of discourse that we are no longer able to take a position of radical iconoclasm.

In face of this almost overwhelming power of the system, the fact of the matter is that we presently have no effective *political* instruments by which to change it. Professor Galbraith's thesis of countervailing power may have worked in former decades; it no longer does. Big government, big business, and big labor are now in consensus. They all work together to maintain the system, and there is no structure of countervailing power to act against the whole. The inadequacy of all present political institutions stands out in bold relief before the Negro in Mississippi related to the Democratic party there, slum dwellers accustomed to the usual types of ward politics, and students and faculty protesting our policy in Vietnam. We simply cannot hope to bring about the type of changes now needed by playing the same old game by the same old rules. But the question remains: is any other type of politics possible?

We may now be ready to face realistically the question that constitutes my fourth point: confronting the power structures. If there is any truth in what I have said thus far, this confrontation is one of the front lines in the struggle for the future of man in a technological society. It represents a long-term contest that will require the total commitment of a new generation, a generation that must be willing, like Moses and the people of Israel, to embark on an exodus. For the battle can be fought only by people who have a new, radical self-identity, individually and collectively. This implies that we must begin very early to lay the foundations for a new style of life, one that combines intense awareness with freedom and independence. We cannot get away from the system, but we can learn to be *in* while not *of* it. We can refuse to take it too seriously or conform with it. And we can help men and women have the type of experience and develop the categories of thought that will permit a fundamental critique of the present order.

Ultimately, what is called for is a new strategy of revolution, a new radical politics. We do not yet know what the shape of this will be, but we may have a few clues. It will, I believe, concentrate at this stage on the formation of small groups of people who are free to search for new perspectives and new solutions, and discover how to create new awareness among the wider public through the use of all possible means of communication by word or parabolic action. It will combine in some way many short battles for small gains with an overall strategy aimed at bringing about basic changes. As I have suggested elsewhere,[2] what we may need today is a *political* equivalent of guerilla warfare.

[2] See Carl Oglesby and Richard Shaull, *Containment and Change,* New York, Macmillan Company, 1967.

REV. WILLIAM J. BYRON, S.J.

12 The Teaching of Business Morality

About ten years ago in the now defunct "Manners and Morals" section of *Time* magazine, an incident was reported which involved essentially the following elements. A woman was driving along a highway and saw a car standing on the shoulder of the road well ahead of her. The driver of the apparently disabled automobile stood by the roadside and signaled to her for help. She pulled off the highway and stopped, whereupon he came up to her, opened the door, pulled her out, and dragged her to the back of her own car where he forced her into the trunk. He locked the trunk, got behind the wheel of his victim's car, and drove her for many miles in many directions before coming to a halt in a quiet, secluded spot. He stepped out of the car and unlocked the trunk. When the abductor turned the handle and lifted the hatch, he was greeted with a shotgun blast fired by his would-be victim. It happened that her husband was a hunting enthusiast and had left a loaded rifle there.

Now, those are the essentials of the story as I recall them. I don't vouch for *Time*'s facts, nor did I attempt to imitate the celebrated *Time* style in presenting them here. My purpose in recounting the event is to relate to it a reflection of my own that it prompted. Wouldn't it liven up an ethics class, I thought, if the dry principles associated with the typical textbook introduction to the "unjust aggressor" could be presented in the context of a story like this? From the reported facts, from the real-life experience, any professor could invite his students to dialogue their way up to the general moral principles.

In teaching undergraduate economics at the University of Maryland, I have used this technique with some success, although both facts and principles are economic, not ethical. The students are told at the beginning of the semester that they will be expected to do a short paper developed from a report in a newspaper or news magazine that relates to any topic covered in the course—fiscal and monetary policy, problems of inflation, unemployment, and so on. The news report is to be clipped and attached to a typewritten essay which links the reported event (for example, a presidential decision to raise or lower taxes) to the appropriate principles as presented in the textbook. My purpose in giving such an assignment is primarily to impress upon the student that the material in his textbook pertains directly to important issues in the off-campus world.

The same device could be used by any theology professor who wished to integrate questions of business morality into his broader course offering. Almost daily there are reports in the press of embezzlement, bribery, conspiracy, extortion, and conflict of interest. Frequently stories of price-fixing and bid-rigging turn up in the news media. Occasionally the public learns that bugs and wiretaps have been used in cases of industrial espionage. The sports pages reveal from time to time that honor has been bought and sold as a result of unhealthy contacts between athletes and gamblers. Ample news coverage is given these days to larger socio-ethical issues like automobile safety, air pollution, and the job-displacement effects of automation. Moral questions raised by technological progress often receive careful journalistic treatment.

The teacher interested in the total moral environment in which his students live and in which their elders earn a living will have frequent occasion to point to moral issues in current events. He cannot depend on *Ramparts* or Ralph Nader or Senator McClellan or Drew Pearson or countless other probers of high or low caliber to rattle ethical skeletons with predictable regularity. But he can expect very few dry spells in the reporting of unethical conduct in matters directly related to business and economic activity. Hence the daily press, the news weeklies, the weekly or biweekly reviews of opinion, and television documentaries combine to form a good source of data. The problems are easy to find. What about the principles?

Let me suggest several ways of presenting the principles, and then let me experiment with several attempts to move from the news report up to the appropriate principle. (I am thinking now in terms of a semester-length course in theology that is not geared exclusively to questions of business morality; nor for that matter need it be a course devoted exclusively to questions of moral theology.) As a source book for moral principles relating to business, both professor and student might want to equip themselves with Thomas M. Garrett's *Business Ethics*.[1] Presumably all could become familiar with this readable and relatively brief text (200 pages) early in the semester. The device, as I said, is to find the moral issue in a news account. Then the student is invited to move back into the text by discussion or written essay. Here are some examples.

Father Garrett's index has several references under "secrecy." He defines a secret as "knowledge which a person has a right and/or an obligation to keep hidden." The more important secrets involve both a right and an obligation to keep the matter hidden. The author divides obligatory secrets into three general categories: (1) the natural secret, (2) the promised secret, and (3) the professional secret. "A comment on each," writes Father Garrett, "will provide us with an analytic tool for handling some of the more common cases in business." [2] He continues:

> The *natural secret* involves knowledge of something which by its nature will cause harm if revealed. . . . Unless there is a *proportionate reason* for revealing the information, such knowledge is to be kept hidden.
>
> Generally speaking, the *promised secret* involves a natural secret. The obligation to keep it, however, arises not only from the nature of the matter, but from the promise or contract by which one binds oneself. . . . Although such secrets are obligatory aside from the nature of the matter, they too may be revealed when silence will cause more harm than good.
>
> The *professional secret* involves not only an implied promise and a natural secret, but the reputation of a group whose services are necessary for society. . . . For this reason, only the most serious reasons can justify the revelation of a professional secret.

[1] Thomas M. Garrett, *Business Ethics*, New York, Appleton-Century-Crofts, 1966.

[2] *Ibid.*, p. 88.

> There may even be cases where a professional man must risk personal ruin rather than violate a trust.[3]

The author acknowledges that in special cases the professional secret may be revealed with proper permission. "Great care and discretion, however, are necessary in the revelation of the professional secret. Unless the fact of permission is known to others, confidence in the profession may still be shaken."[4]

Since any theory is a frame within which one examines facts, a student who knows even this little bit of ethical theory about secrets could well have absorbed into such a framework the following headline on page 1 of the *Washington Post* of November 30, 1966: "Judge Backs Mute Stand of Newsman." The story related the following facts: a grand jury in a suburban Washington county was investigating alleged zoning irregularities. Walter J. Sheridan, an investigative reporter for NBC News, was subpoenaed by the grand jury but refused to answer questions about a conversation he had some months before with one Kenneth A. Patrick, a former employee of a then deceased but still central figure in the grand jury's inquiry. Mr. Sheridan claimed he obtained the information the grand jury wanted in his capacity as a news reporter, and that it was therefore "privileged" or confidential. As he put it, he had talked with Patrick "in confidence, off the record, as a newsman."

Sheridan was ordered to appear before a circuit court judge the next day to show cause why he should not be held in contempt of the grand jury. The circuit court judge upheld the newsman's position, saying in effect that the law protects the privacy of conversations between newsmen and their sources in the same way as other laws protect conversations between physicians and patients, lawyers and clients, and priests and penitents. The reference is to Maryland law. In their arguments before the circuit judge, Mr. Sheridan's attorneys used the line of reasoning and even some of the same vocabulary that your students will find in Garrett's text. They argued that "The greater freedom of the press is more important to the long-run welfare of the people of Maryland than an occasional forced disclosure of a confidential communication to a reporter."

[3] *Ibid.*, pp. 88-89.
[4] *Ibid.*

All of this received detailed newspaper and television coverage. The route to the principles is evident. One may object that a newsman is not ordinarily considered a businessman and that this is not directly a matter of business morality. My reply would be that the principles are the same, and just keep your eye on the headlines for a story more clearly focused on the businessman.

Our moral menu has much to offer for discussion and analysis in the area of corruption. Here again, it is not always easy to isolate businessmen from politicians, public officials, and labor leaders. But many questions of business morality come into sharp focus if one has a tool for the analysis of bribery and related forms of corruption. For such a tool I would suggest an article of mine which appeared in the *Catholic Mind* in June, 1964, under the title of "The Graft Syndrome." My purpose in publishing it then and in referring to it now was to make available once again an analytical tool presented in *Theological Studies* by Father John C. Ford, S.J., in 1945. Father Ford discussed the problem we still face of educating the consciences of businessmen and politicians to the sinfulness of many common practices. Instead of defining graft (Webster does that adequately enough), he offered a threefold test designed to detect its presence: if one finds a combination of (1) secrecy, (2) easy money, and (3) the violation of a trust, one can reasonably conclude that graft is present and that there is something sinful in the transaction. For closer analysis, Father Ford provided the three degrees of graft: the gift, the bribe, and the holdup (extortion).

An excellent description of extortion was given during the NBC-TV three-and-a-half-hour special on organized crime in August, 1966. Austin Perlow of the *Long Island Press* was asked, "Why do you think organized crime is so interested in getting into these labor unions?" His reply: "It is a beautiful weapon—shakedown and extortion. Look how easy it is. You got an employer, a big employer. You say, 'Look, Jack, I think we're gonna have a strike here next week.' And he says, 'A strike! My God, with all these contracts to fill! I'm gonna be sued—I have half a million dollars in contracts. You're gonna close me down. I'll go out of business; I'll be sued.' The answer's very easy: 'Well, maybe we can avoid a strike. I think if I had a couple of dollars to pass out among the guys, they'd see the light. Ah, let's say, ah, about five grand under the table, and I'll get the guys to talk it over, and maybe they won't want to strike after that.' That is extortion."

The chief element in any graft situation is the violation of trust. Give the student Father Ford's three-part model, and he has a tool that he can use when he picks up the paper and reads an item like the following lead in a wire service story datelined Baton Rouge, October 18, 1966. "FBI agents arrested and charged a Baton Rouge barber today with attempting to bribe three-fourths of the Louisiana State University backfield to shave points and control six football games." Reading on into the story, the student will look for indications of secrecy and easy money, and then he will reflect on the nature of the trust that is violated in the process.

If the student resides or studies in Washington, D. C., he is located in one of the fastest-growing metropolitan areas in the United States. Building activity there is brisk; pressure to re-zone suburban land for high-rise apartment units, shopping centers, trailer camps, and so on is very great. It is not by accident that grand juries in each of the three suburban counties surrounding the District of Columbia—Fairfax in Virginia and Montgomery and Prince Georges in Maryland—have recently considered the involvement of county officials and land developers in the alleged offering and accepting of bribes to insure the desired re-zoning of land. As of this writing, indictments have been brought in in two of these three jurisdictions, and in one county convictions are already in.

On Tuesday, February 21, 1967, readers of the *Washington Post* learned that "John P. Parrish, a suspended Fairfax County supervisor, and Isidore Parzov, a land developer, were found guilty yesterday by an Alexandria Federal Court jury of bribery and conspiracy in a rezoning action . . . that permitted construction of the Bradlick Shopping Center in Annandale." The prosecution successfully argued that Parzov bribed Parrish to vote for the re-zoning by giving him 1,000 shares of stock, valued at $5,250, in the company developing the center. Fuller accounts of the story reveal the elements of secrecy, and little reflection is needed to detect the violation of a trust when a public official sells his vote.

For a third source of principles, we turn to authoritative Church teaching. One principle of social ethics that can also be called a moral principle in a properly theological sense, since it is enunciated in authoritative Church teaching, is that of subsidiarity. This can be stated simply, and should be incorporated into the student's moral tool kit.

> This supremely important principle of social philosophy, one which cannot be set aside or altered, remains firm and unshaken: Just as it is wrong to withdraw from the individual and commit to the community at large what private enterprise and endeavor can accomplish, so it is likewise unjust and a gravely harmful disturbance of right order to turn over to a greater society of higher rank functions and services which can be performed by lesser bodies on a lower plane. For a social undertaking of any sort, by its very nature, ought to aid the members of the body social, but never to destroy and absorb them.[5]

Applying the principle of subsidiarity is no simple matter. But attempts to apply it will carry classroom discussion into contact with most of our contemporary social problems. Let us take just one example: air pollution. The takeoff point for a discussion of this issue could have been the January 27, 1967, cover story in *Time*, or the daily press coverage of Health, Education and Welfare Secretary John W. Gardner's speech at the Third National Conference on Air Pollution, held in Washington in December of 1966. Secretary Gardner said:

> Our concern is not merely with a suffocating haze that offends our senses, that soils laundry and buildings, that damages crops and corrodes metal. We are dealing with a killer. People become sick and they die from breathing dirty air. . . . Our choices are narrow. We can remain indoors and live like moles for an unspecified number of days each year. We can issue gas masks to a large segment of the population. We can live in doomed cities. Or we can take action to stop fouling the air we breathe.

Moral question: Who takes the action? Where is the obligation? On the owner of the air-polluting family car, or on those who build that car? On the owners of the air-polluting fleet of diesel-powered city buses, or on those who ride the buses? What is the obligation of those who own or manage the complicated operations that lie beneath our huge industrial smokestacks? What are the obligations of lawmakers, taxpayers, consumers, producers? The

[5] Pius XI, *Quadragesimo anno*, *AAS*, XXIII (1931), 203; quoted in John XXIII, *Mater et magistra*, *AAS*, LIII (1961), 414.

moral question is an amalgam of what, when, how, and at whose expense.

In the same broad context of subsidiarity, discussion will emerge on auto safety, retraining of the unemployed, foreign economic assistance, and most other current issues.

I have not discussed television at any length as a possible source. Most of the problems I have mentioned have been laid out rather well in documentaries on the commercial and also the educational networks. For instance, CBS News did an hour-long special on air pollution recently. NBC's three-and-a-half-hour special on organized crime pointed out many links between organized crime and American business. One problem with television programs is that they tend to be highly perishable. You see a show once and you ordinarily don't have easy access to the script or to a repeat viewing. But many public libraries circulate TV documentaries from their film desks; they can be obtained for classroom or discussion club use.

I want to make one final reference that will help us attune ourselves to the problem side—that is, to the moral concerns businessmen say they actually have, as distinguished from (although not necessarily opposed to) the problems theologians think they should have. Father Raymond C. Baumhart, S.J., has done a lot of work in this area,[6] having begun his investigation in his doctoral dissertation at the Harvard Business School. In a recent article, Father Baumhart specifies seven problem areas which teachers and students of business morality might want to think about in connection with related items in the press. Remember, now, that these are the moral problems conscientious businessmen face and about which they seek moral advice:

1. Hiring and firing.
2. Commercial bribery (gifts, entertainment).
3. Honesty:
   a. In advertising.
   b. In tax returns.
   c. In expense accounts.
   d. In insurance claims.

[6] See Raymond C. Baumhart, "How Ethical Are Businessmen?", *Harvard Business Review*, July-August, 1961; his articles in *America*, January 6, February 3, and April 14, 1962, collected in the pamphlet "Ethics of the Businessman," New York, America Press, Fall, 1962; and "The Theologian and Moral Problems of Businessmen," *Homiletic and Pastoral Review*, September, 1966.

4. Cheating the customers.
5. Pricing.
6. Conflicts of loyalty to country and company.
7. Primacy of solvency for a corporation.

These are somewhat specialized problems, but students who go into business can expect to encounter them, and should therefore be helped to prepare themselves. But it would be wrong to keep the moral focus too specific. It is the societal sense, the social conscience that is the object of formation in business morality. This is not an easy thing to do, from the side of the teacher or the student. In 1959, Cardinal Montini, now Pope Paul VI, put his finger on the precise point of the difficulty when he addressed a group of businessmen in Milan: "It is far easier to speak of the solution of social questions to the working classes than it is to you; to them the solution promises improvements, but from you it demands sacrifices."

V The Religious Phenomenon of Sex in a Secular Age

And Ozias and the ancients said to her: All things which thou hast spoken are true; and there is nothing to be reprehended in thy words.
Now therefore pray for us; for thou art a holy woman, and one fearing God.

JUDITH 8:28-29

PAULINE L. TURNER

13 The Contribution of Women to Theology

Human beings are meant for community. They are persons, meant to share consciousness, freedom, and human development. The very possibility of such sharing necessitates distinctiveness and complementarity. True human community is grounded in communications. These two factors, of distinctiveness and complementarity, make human personal communication possible.[1]

The polarity between men and women is certainly one of the most basic complementarities which make human community what it is and which point to what it might become.[2] It is the basis of the nuclear community which is the family. The same polarity affects other communities of human persons deeply, whether by its presence or by its absence.

The community which is of direct concern here is the faith community which is the Church. In this instance, community is established by a sharing, a communication, of faith consciousness. Hence distinct and complementary faith insights and faith experience must be shared by those who make up the people of God. By this sharing, the members of the Church are meant to become

[1] See Louis Lavelle, *Evil and Suffering*, New York, Macmillan Company, 1963, pp. 93-159; and Maurice Nedoncelle, *Love and the Person*, New York, Sheed & Ward, 1966, where the point is made that "to be oneself one must be at least two" (p. 234).

[2] Care must be exercised in the meaning we ascribe to such terms as *polarity* and *complementarity* in the context of transsubjective relationships. Abel Janniere offers important clarifications in Chapter 8, "The Confrontation of Man and Woman as Dialogue and History," of his book *The Anthropology of Sex*, New York, Harper & Row, Publishers, 1967.

more deeply united one to another, and the corporate faith life of the Church is meant to advance.[3]

That the relation between man and woman is of central importance in the faith life of the Church seems indicated by revelation. From the viewpoint of the priestly tradition in Genesis 1:27, we find an indication that the reflection of the mystery of God in the life of man is intimately linked with the relationship of man and woman: "So God created man in his own image, in the image of God he created him; male and female he created them."

But if this Old Testament insight seems somewhat vague as a basis for discussion, the role of the sacrament of marriage in the continuing process of Christian revelation makes it inescapably clear that the reality of the Church as a community is revealed and effected by the community of man and woman in marriage.[4]

This means that the Church's evolving comprehension of faith is dependent upon men's and women's sharing their understanding with one another. Since theology is the ordered and creative advance in the understanding of faith, it seems necessary that men and women participate in an exchange at this level. The role of women in theology is essential to any *integral* growth of theology. It is about this one aspect, among many, of woman's role in the Church that I wish to make a few remarks.

I would suggest that an exploration of woman's special theological contribution is connected with her Christian experience of being a woman. There are large areas of theological process where she shares with her male colleagues the careful gathering of material and the utilization of the different methodologies. As a working thesis, however, I propose that her own *conscious existence as a woman,* which is the matrix for all her human and Christian experience and reflection, enables the woman theologian to make a unique contribution to the discipline.

[3] Bernard Cooke, "Theology of Communication," an unpublished paper; Henri de Lubac, *The Splendor of the Church,* Glen Rock, N. J., Paulist Press, 1963, pp. 11-32; and Karl Rahner, "The Development of Dogma," *Theological Investigations,* vol. I: *God, Christ, Mary, and Grace,* Baltimore, Helicon Press, 1961, pp. 39-78, and "Considerations on the Development of Dogma," *Theological Investigations,* vol. IV: *More Recent Writings,* Baltimore, Helicon Press, 1967, pp. 3-35.

[4] Edward Schillebeeckx, *Marriage: Human Reality and Saving Mystery,* New York, Sheed & Ward, 1965.

This approach is linked with a very important development in contemporary theology, one made possible by man's increased awareness of his states of consciousness: the use of the analogue of human experience to elucidate the mysteries of faith. Reflection on the different experiences of human beings as they live in relation to one another enables the theologian to understand better what it is that God is doing in their lives. Piet Fransen analyzes the historical development of Christian theology and points out that three basic methodologies have been operative: the psychological, the essential, and the existential.[5] In the present discussion, we are concerned with the implications of existential methodology for our subject. Besides such undoubted advantages as both its adaptability to our ways of thought and language today and its facility for illuminating the Hebraic thought patterns in which revelation in the Old and New Testaments is cast, existential methodology ". . . expounds an understanding of the being of man which has affinity with the understanding of his being implicit in the thought of the biblical writers." [6]

Fransen gives us this definition of existential analysis in its strict sense:

> [It is] the systematic exposition of the necessary a priori conditions for the possibility of a given real existence in the wholeness of its human situation. . . .
>
> It attempts to follow as closely as possible the flowing life of our actual existence in its real human situation, and this not from the outside, as in a description of the many-colored variety of our psychological life, but from the inside. . . . It considers our existence as a whole in its personal authenticity, in its dialectical tension between the spiritual unity of our personal liberty and the multiplicity of our existence in time and space.[7]

The importance of using this method in theologizing today is further underlined by Mary Rose Barral in her study of the philosophy of Merleau-Ponty:

> No reflection on a doctrine will be adequate if it remains divorced from existential experience. . . . Existential experience is the

[5] Piet Fransen, "Three Ways of Dogmatic Thought," *Cross Currents*, Spring, 1963, pp. 129-148.

[6] John Macquarrie, *An Existentialist Theology*, New York, Harper & Row, Publishers, 1965, p. 18.

[7] Fransen, *op. cit.*, pp. 142-143.

"being-to-the-world" of man himself, his belonging to the world, his being committed to his situation. Therefore, I cannot really reflect on a doctrine and make it mine by assimilating its meaning unless I "live it" in some way.[8]

An important instance of the influence of this mentality can be seen in our present understanding of sacramental action.[9] We are moving away from a tendency to understand *ex opere operato* as magical or automatic.[10] Instead we are stressing the transformation of consciousness effected by symbol.[11] Not only in sacramental theology but in every area of theology today the element of consciousness is in the forefront of theological speculation. One need only mention a few examples to bear this out. In Christology, we are examining the nature and development of human conscious experience.[12] In eschatology, we are asking what our human consciousness in the next life will be.[13] If human consciousness requires a bodily way of being, what does this say about our understanding of the mystery of the risen body?[14] What new light is thrown on trinitarian theology by the unity of the three Persons as one shared consciousness? [15] Since it is clear from these examples how heavily theology is drawing upon consciousness and experience, it seems

[8] Mary Rose Barral, *The Role of the Body-Subject in Interpersonal Relations,* Pittsburgh, Duquesne University Press, 1965, p. 38.

[9] Karl Rahner, *Church and Sacraments,* New York, Herder and Herder, 1963.

[10] Bernard Cooke, "The Sacraments as the Continuing Acts of Christ," in *Proceedings of the Sixteenth Annual Convention of the Catholic Theological Society of America,* pp. 42-68.

[11] Bernard Cooke, "Theology of Imagination," in *Focus: A Theological Journal* (Regis College), 1966, pp. 7-16; Karl Rahner, "The Theology of Symbol" and "The Word and the Eucharist," *Theological Investigations,* Vol. IV, pp. 221-252, 253-286.

[12] Engelbert Gutwenger, "The Problem of Christ's Knowledge," in *Concilium,* vol. XI: *Who Is Jesus of Nazareth?,* Glen Rock, N. J., Paulist Press, 1966, pp. 91-105; and Karl Rahner, "The Enfleshment of God," *Spiritual Exercises,* New York, Herder and Herder 1965, pp. 97-113, and "Dogmatic Reflections on the Knowledge and Self-Consciousness of Christ," *Theological Investigations,* vol. V: *Church and History,* Baltimore, Helicon Press, 1965, pp. 157-215.

[13] Bernard Cooke, "Heaven," in *Proceedings of the Twenty-Third National Liturgical Week,* Seattle, 1962, pp. 94-99; Ladislaus Boros, *The Mystery of Death,* New York, Herder and Herder, 1965.

[14] Karl Rahner, "The Resurrection of the Body," *Theological Investigations,* vol. II: *Man in the Church,* Baltimore, Helicon Press, 1964, pp. 203-216.

[15] Cooke, "Theology of Communication," unpublished paper.

critically important that *all* of humankind's variety of experiences flow into our theological process.[16]

If we examine the historical development of theology, including the present-day situation, we find a twofold limitation on the theological process. Not only has the experience drawn upon been almost exclusively that of men, but this was further narrowed to the experience of men involved in the clerical state. Not only does our present theology represent and reflect the masculine experience in the Christian community, but in large measure it is influenced deeply by both the clerical and celibate status of these theologians.

One becomes aware of how the complete absence of women from theology may have caused a grave lacuna when one reflects on the theological process intrinsic in Scripture itself. The final inspired text as we have it is the result of the interactions of many complementary understandings of faith. This interplay of mentalities gives a richness to biblical thought even though the feminine mind is scarcely represented. It would seem, then, that a well-rounded evolution of Christian theology should complement the traditional masculine cast of past centuries with the viewpoint of the educated Christian woman.

The commitment to a role in Christian life and the celibate disposition of one's sexuality are both radical elements which necessarily ground and condition one's experience as Christian. For as Father Karl Rahner says:

> The sexual character of human beings is not merely one limited sector of their existence, such as would make it relevant to religion only insofar as that sector is subject to particular moral norms. Sexual character governs the being and life of the whole person (though in varying ways and with varying intensities) in all dimensions. One is a man or a woman in every situation.[17]

Marc Oraison says much the same from a psychiatric point of view:

> No human being can react to and adapt to his surrounding world except his behavior proceed elementally from his very real sexuality. . . .

[16] Bernard Cooke, "The Existential Pertinence of Religion," in *Concilium*, vol. XVIX: *Spirituality in the Secular City*, Glen Rock, N. J., Paulist Press, 1966, pp. 17-22.

[17] Karl Rahner, *Theology for Renewal*, New York, Sheed & Ward, 1964, p. 58.

> While sexual reality does not create the specific nature of human consciousness, it does serve as a basic essential condition for the direction which developing consciousness takes.[18]

It would seem that no matter how honestly and sincerely the male theologian in the Church tries to bring the *full* spectrum of Christian experience to bear on the process of theologizing, the limiting factor of his own masculinity dooms him to failure.

There has been a remarkable absence on the theological scene of the laity, and especially women, with their life experiences, their points of view, their states of consciousness. These have not functioned as the principle of interpreting the Christian experience. Yet we are becoming aware that this Christian form of life is an unavoidable point of entry into understanding the mysteries of faith.[19] From sacramental actions, we come to know the reality of the Church; in terms of the Church, we understand the present reality of Christ. Since our faith response to Christ is intrinsically dependent for its authenticity on the quality of our faith, we can begin to see the gravity of a situation where the understanding of faith is based on the narrow experience which we have just described. Unless we draw upon the total Christian community's experience of faith, we will continue to have a truncated theology.

The woman who functions as a theologian inevitably does so as a woman: "Since in the religious sphere it is the whole man to whom the summons comes, and who has got to arrive at fulfillment, it cannot but be the case that he has to work out his salvation as that concrete whole which he is; and thus as a man or as a woman." [20]

But what are the special elements in the perceptive substratum of a woman that would give her a particular point of view with regard to the mysteries of faith? Woman is a spirit existing in the world bodily; and so reflection upon the bodily nature of humans might throw some light on the consciousness proper to woman.

By way of summary of the role of the body for the human person, we might single out three functions: the body is the dimension of the human being that (1) locates one in time and

[18] Marc Oraison, *The Human Mystery of Sexuality*, New York, Sheed & Ward, 1967, pp. 8, 21.

[19] Jean Mouroux, *The Christian Experience*, New York, Sheed & Ward, 1954.

[20] Rahner, *Theology for Renewal*, *op. cit.*, p. 58.

space, (2) translates the invisible aspects of one's being into the visible order, and (3) is a means for executing one's intentions and plans. These three functions can be subsumed under what we could characterize as the *raison d'être* and dignity of the body: the condition of the presence of one human person to another person, and thereby one's presence to oneself.[21]

If bodily existence is the condition of the presence of one person to another, then bodily differences point to a somewhat different mode and experience of presence. The function of bodily differences which are intrinsically linked with sexuality is pointed out by Philippe Muller:

> The individual, who always tends to close in on himself, as if he were the totality, is opened by sexuality to his fellows, and even more, the future. Thus, at the center of the individual, sexuality is the sign of his incompleteness, if he wishes to measure himself against the rest of the world; it is the inner presence of his own contradiction of this other, which is life, and also of this other which is species. Thus, sexuality manifests the fundamental "ec-centricity" of every individual, taking the term in its literal sense. It is at the human level that the problematic of sexuality will burst forth, where it is no longer simply a biological consciousness straining to escape its condition. Moreover, it is not simply a relation to these other selves, which each of us has in his present and future fellows. It is the basic presence of the other at the center of my existence, a presence accepted, denied, elusive, pre-conscious, hidden or manifest.[22]

It should perhaps be pointed out that such differences do not indicate that the contribution of woman in theology will be either inferior or superior to that of man. Rather, it should be viewed as complementary. Theologically, the battle of the sexes was laid to rest by Saint Paul: "As many of you as have been baptized in Christ have put on Christ . . . there is neither male nor female; for you are all one in Christ Jesus." [23]

Karl Rahner comments on the meaning of this passage from Galatians:

> In the realm of the truth of the Gospel and the redeeming grace of God, neither man nor woman has any priority as far as concerns

[21] See Lavelle, "The Open Consciousness," *op. cit.*, pp. 117-120; Barral, *op. cit.*

[22] Philippe Muller, quoted in Paul Ricoeur, "Wonder, Eroticism, and Enigma," *Cross Currents*, Spring, 1964, p. 149.

[23] Gal. 3:27-28.

> the eternal salvation of human beings. In relation to the ultimate question of salvation, to the total decision of life, there is no difference between the sexes. In this respect, no one has any advantage by being a man or being a woman.[24]

We have already indicated that a basis for the complementarity of man and woman is found in the pages of Scripture as early as Genesis 1:27; Ephesians 5 points up the profound sacramentality of that situation. The different biological and cultural backgrounds of women in their experience of reality enable them to make specific contributions to the advance of theology, contributions which would not be possible without the reflection of the feminine experience on the mysteries of faith.

At this point, the question might be raised whether woman's place in society is hereditary or culturally determined.[25] A few remarks may help clarify this point. The metaphysical view of each man as an incarnate spirit points to the *uniqueness* of each human individual. To describe any individual woman as a particular concrete expression of the "eternal feminine" seems to be an appeal to the realm of Platonic ideas to explain the difference between the sexes. The result is disastrous—the individual feminine person is deprived of her uniqueness.

Implied in the notion of man as an embodied spirit is the idea that the body is the sacrament of the spirit; it is the spirit which determines and specifies the form of the body. If we look at it philosophically, the fact that there are two bodily expressions of humanity, male and female, indicates an intrinsic link between the spiritual aspect of human being and the sexuality of the body which sacramentalizes the human person.

But if the body is a sacrament of the spirit, and, as is obvious, the bodies of man and woman complement one another in the bodily realm, does this not point to a complementarity in every dimension of their being? Or to reverse the point: there is bodily complementarity between man and woman precisely because of the mutuality in the spiritual sphere. This mutuality—or complementarity—between man and woman, however, does not in any way preclude equality one with another. Women share with men the right to become fully human, to develop their personhood, to be-

[24] Rahner, *Theology for Renewal, op. cit.*, pp. 57-58.

[25] A study of the contrasting views of the "environmentalist" and "eternal feminine" schools can be found in Sydney Callahan, *The Illusion of Eve*, New York, Sheed & Ward, 1965, pp. 13-34.

come who they are. Included in this right is the right to be different, the right to be unique, the right to live in expression of one's sexuality. It needs to be emphasized that not only are these rights which women have, but they are responsibilities of the first order. To misconstrue equality to mean "sameness" with men would hold the danger of leading to a situation where the polarity of the sexes would disappear.

In the last analysis, many questions remain unanswered. We barely understand the precise nature of the irreducible element of uniqueness which functions as a matrix for women's conscious experience and for the delineation of her distinctiveness from men. While we await and welcome scientific studies which will clarify these questions, it is important that the obvious fact of complementarity be more and more recognized and implemented in the concrete order. There is no area of human knowledge, living, and endeavor which will not be enriched by the presence of both poles of humanity working together in cooperation.

Any worthwhile discussion of this point must deal with this question in the concrete. We are talking about woman's contribution at a specific historical point in the development of the Church, the present moment. Whether the differences of experience which we have described are intrinsic to woman as woman or whether they are the results of historico-cultural conditioning, the experience today is different, and women do presently reflect the action of the mystery of grace in half of the human race. For that reason, it is evident that the Christian experience of woman ought to pass into the theological process.

One area critical to our discussion is that of intellectual processes. Recent studies of the nature of the intellectual processes in girls and women seem to point to the conclusion that many of the differences actually discernible may be grounded in the way girls are educated rather than in some psychological characteristic. Dr. Eleanor Maccoby, associate professor of psychology at Stanford University, states that

> . . . girls on the average develop a somewhat different way of handling incoming information . . . their thinking is less analytical, more global, and more preservative—and this . . . may serve them very well for many kinds of functioning, but it is not the kind of thinking that is most conducive to high-level intellectual productivity, especially in science. . . . There are many women who

> think analytically, and many men do not, but there are consistent differences in the average performances of the two sexes. . . .

Dr. Maccoby goes on to assert that this may not be due to a feminine quality of the intellect but to the way women are educated for personhood:

> . . . intellectual development does not occur as a kind of isolated "unfolding" process obeying its own inner laws, but rather . . . it is responsive, in some degree, to the *nature of the network of interpersonal relations* [italics added] in which the child is involved, and . . . certain modes of thought may depend on the development of certain aspects of the person that we have previously thought of as "personality" rather than qualities of the intellect.

Noting that research in this area is only beginning, Dr. Maccoby points out that recent studies indicate the emergence of consistent trends wherein the "Key to the matter seems to lie in whether, and how soon, a child is encouraged to assume initiative, to take responsibility for himself, and to solve problems by himself, rather than rely upon others for the direction of his activities." [26]

It seems, then, that the woman who is encouraged to develop to the full all the powers of her personhood in interaction with other persons may find analytic modes of thought as natural to her as the "intuitive," which has been thought to be her peculiar preserve. Only when such a situation has been in fact achieved can the genuine differences and complementarities of men and women be thoroughly investigated.

In the meantime, the growing availability of higher studies in theology is providing women with the opportunity to theologize in the Church. This means that women can now begin seriously the process of enriching theology with their own special insights, lacking which theology would continue to remain incomplete. The task of rethinking centuries of theology as well as building an integral theology in the present and future challenges today's woman in the Church.

[26] Dr. Eleanor Maccoby, "Woman's Intellect," in *The Potential of Women: A Symposium,* New York, McGraw-Hill Book Company, 1963, pp. 31-33. Dr. Maccoby bases her conclusions on studies indicating that a child at age six whose IQ will increase in the next four years will be competitive, self-assertive, independent, and dominant in interaction with other children, while the children who will show declining IQs during the next four years are children who are passive, shy, and dependent.

SISTER JANE STIER, O.S.U.

14 Women in the Church

My own experience as a woman in the Church has been such in recent times I am almost tempted to say that we have a false problem here—that we are creating an issue where there is none. I know a number of great women in the Church, both sisters and laywomen, who are making a real contribution to the betterment of people's lives. They teach in universities, write books, give lectures; rear intelligent, active, and good children—or ones not so intelligent, active, or good; encourage and make their husbands happy; and have all the involvement in church life they could possibly want or handle. Woman's contribution to church life in both past and present history in the United States has been so great that one begins to wonder where the problem lies. Why worry about women in the Church—where would it be without us?

And yet, as with so many other aspects of church life, past and present, women's contribution is in spite of existing church structures, not because of them. A recent incident exemplifies one facet of the issue. Two sisters were standing in line before a theater where *Alfie* was being shown. A woman in front of them turned around and said, "Oh, sisters, you don't want to come in here. This is an *adult* movie."

This is a minor example of what some of us have experienced in other ways. Some lay people as well as churchmen have simply written out of adult life one group of women in the Church. They will grant that sisters have a place in the Church, as minders of children, teachers, or writers, but let sisters stay out of the real world of adult human experience.

I mentioned this incident recently to a group of adult laymen and laywomen. Most of them thought that sisters ought not see the movie. I haven't seen it, as a matter of fact, but my opinion, which I expressed then, is that a sister might have as much reason for seeing it as would any adult woman. The implication that we should not seems to imply that we should not know about sex or cannot understand it.

Certain historical events lead to an understanding of why sisters in the Church are thought of as less than adult. In the early Church, three groups of women had recognized status: widows, deaconesses, and virgins. The first two groups disappeared early in church history, leaving the official church structure to men. The role of the virgin came to be associated with the development of monasticism, so that around the fifth century, virginity lived in monastic communities was the only official form of church life for women.

Rules for religious women were written by men, a practice which continues with rare exception to the present day. Between the seventh and tenth centuries, women in Anglo-Saxon and Germanic societies were active within and outside the monasteries. Aside from this period, society has been largely male-dominated.

The Renaissance era meant more education and consequently greater freedom for women. Angela Merici founded an uncloistered community of women in Brescia, Italy, in 1534, and hers was the first rule written by a woman for women in the western Church. Angela's daughters outside Italy were to feel the effect of the Tridentine reform, however, and they, like the other religious women of the time, became *moniales*, or nuns. This meant they lived behind cloister walls under solemn vows; this condition changed Angela's original idea, which had deliberately broken from the traditional forms of religious life.

The struggle of Vincent de Paul and Mary Ward to found uncloistered communities of women to meet the social needs of the seventeenth century also illustrates the problem. Vincent de Paul used subterfuge and great ingenuity to keep his Daughters of Charity from confinement behind the grille. The French bishops generally considered that religious life for women meant withdrawal from the world, cloister, divine office, and traditional community practices. To Vincent, it meant meeting the needs of the people of his time.

Mary Ward, who knew from first-hand experience what she was talking about, had this to say to her sisters regarding the seventeenth-century churchman's attitude toward women:

> Heretofore we have been told by men we must believe. It is true we must, but let us be wise, and know what we are to believe and what not, and not be made to think we can do nothing. . . . Wherein are we so inferior to other creatures that they should term us but women? . . . There was a Father that lately came into England whom I heard say that he would not for a thousand of worlds be a woman, because he thought a woman could not apprehend God. I answered nothing, but only smiled, although I could have answered him, by the experience I have of the contrary. . . . His want is in experience.[1]

The situation hasn't changed too much even at the present time. Religious life continues in large measure to be regulated by men. The fact that Archbishop Paul J. Hallinan of Atlanta proposed during the fourth session of Vatican II in 1965 that women be represented in the Congregation of Religious shows that we don't have much more to say about our life now than did the women of post-Tridentine France. He, by the way, was one of seventeen bishops to speak at Vatican II for an improved status for women in the Church. In spite of his proposal, there are no women in the Congregation of Religious. Nor are there women on the Commission established for the implementation of Vatican II's decree for religious, although the United States Conference of Major Superiors requested in 1965 that religious sisters be represented. Religious sisters still appeal to a Roman Congregation for such minor practices as making a change in their religious habit.

Perhaps the fact that our religious life is male-regulated is largely the fault of us women. We don't accomplish on a large intercommunity scale what individual sisters and communities are doing: simply subordinating the structures of their lives to the needs of the apostolate.

In other words, I think that it is in the area of church structures themselves where change has to be made. Individual sisters are leading adult human lives, making a real contribution to the Church of this century. But they are doing this within a general church

[1] Mary Chambers, *Life of Mary Ward,* London, Burns and Oates, 1882-1885, pp. 410-411.

organization that hasn't drastically changed since the post-Tridentine reform era. Whenever a woman does something in the official Church, it has major news value. The role of women in the Church will be a matter of our concern until the time when a woman or her work or her ideas can be chosen not because she is a woman but because she has a contribution to make in a particular area. And this, I think, will only come about when the structure is so altered that women are in the organizational setup of the Church on all levels.

An example of what I mean is this. Rosemary Goldie was recently named an undersecretary of the Commission on the Lay Apostolate. She is the first woman to be appointed to an administrative post in the Vatican, and the news is world-shaking. We'll only really be able to make a contribution to the Church when we are taken on our own merits as persons and not as special people because we are women.

I think very few men are ready for this. It may be that women also aren't yet ready for this, but our unpreparedness has something to do with the attitude of men toward us. A layman on the faculty of the university where I teach told me that he didn't mind a few women on the faculty just so there weren't too many. One of my sophomore students answered this outlook well: he said that most of the fellows don't care whether the teacher is a man or a woman; what they care about is his or her competency in the field being taught. Until we reach this attitude in the Church regarding any and all positions, women will not have full equality.

I do not include in this at the present time the question of ordination to the priesthood. I think that for psychological, cultural, and sociological reasons, we are not ready for woman priests and bishops in this country. What I am speaking of are areas other than those directly related to preaching in Church and presiding at the eucharistic celebration. If society in the United States evolves to this point in the future, if it already has elsewhere, I would have no problem with the idea of a woman priest.

Two recent studies by male theologians, José A. Idigoras Goya, S.J., at the Pontifical Catholic University in Lima, Peru, and Haye van der Meer, S.J., at Innsbruck, have shown that there is no theological argument against the ordination of women. That the poor have the gospel preached to them seems more important than the sex of the priest. But at present in this country, I think that in all areas other than the priesthood women need to be considered on an equal level with men.

We need to put an end right away and once and for all to the mentality that sees woman as man's temptress, the eternal Eve, waiting to ensnare him. This attitude has been evident in the history of religious orders, where the cloister has been imposed on women so that they would not be a temptation to men. The result has been sexlessness as the goal of religious living for sisters. Instead of seeing our femininity as a central aspect of our persons, we have tended until recently to try to disguise it with heavy shoes, man-sized handkerchiefs, headdresses which cover the hair and mask one's face. Enforced isolation of women religious has to be stopped entirely. If we are going to be college teachers or women involved in the social or educational apostolates of the Church, we are as much in need of the other experiences of life as are men. I mean plainly and simply that we need contacts with men and women involved in similar work as much as men do. One still occasionally meets the mentality that will accept all kinds of work from a sister provided it doesn't make her step out of the traditional structure of her convent.

It may seem that I have equated the question of the role of women in the Church with that of the religious sister. I do think the two are connected: if the sisters can break through the long tradition that has defeminized them and has treated them as less than equal to man, I feel certain this will enhance the role of women in the Church generally. As a college teacher, I believe our problems are very similar to those of the laywomen on our faculties.

I seem also to have equated the problem of women in the Church with the official church structure. Mention should be made of the fact that women are playing a major role in the life of the Church whenever and wherever they are leading adult Christian lives. In this postconciliar age, it would be a mistake to equate woman's contribution to the Church with that made within the official church structure.

Two facts indicate that women today have a better chance of clarifying their role in the Church both for themselves and for others than have women in the past. One is the improved status of woman generally: our counterparts in secular society are obtaining recognition in practically all areas of life. The second is the greater understanding we have today of the positive aspect of sexuality, of the fact that one's sexuality is engaged in all areas of his or her life and that fruitfulness depends on the association of men and women in their work.

One final point: as I see it, we need to look for no single answer to the problem of woman's role in the Church. Each woman has to face the complexities of her own situation. Real competency in one's field, whether one is a man or a woman, will hardly go unnoticed. In those cases in which a woman exercises her competency while expressing a deep regard for her womanliness, that is, without imitating men but manifesting her own womanly style, I think we have taken the biggest step forward: a step toward building the Church as a community of love made up of men and women, a Church which manifests the impress of both masculinity and femininity on all levels of activity.

EDWARD J. FOYE

15 The Androgynous Church

In all probability, mankind's first conceptualization of deity was under the form of the feminine: as the *magna mater*, productive of all things.[1] Perhaps it was because primitive man had not yet glimpsed the role of the male principle in the reproductive process. Bronislaw Malinowski has shown that among the Trobriand Islanders, the "official" doctrine concerning human generation is that the women are fecundated by the spirits and the male really has nothing to do with it.[2] A similar unawareness exists among the aboriginal people of Australia,[3] and lest we feel ourselves too sophisticated, let me include the experience of a medical social worker of my acquaintance who had worked in Appalachia. She was interviewing a lady who was having more children than the family had means

[1] See especially Erich Neumann, *The Great Mother: An Analysis of the Archetype*, tr. Ralph Manheim, New York, Pantheon Books, 1955; and his *The Origins and History of Consciousness*, 2 vols., tr. R. F. C. Hull, Bollingen Series, New York, Pantheon Books, 1954; Harper & Row, Publishers, Harper Torchbooks, 1962. In general, see Sir James Frazer's *The Golden Bough: A Study in Magic and Religion*, various editions; Joseph Campbell, *The Masks of God: Primitive Mythology*, New York, Viking Press, 1959. See as well the remarkable vision of Mother Isis in Apuleius' *Golden Ass* (ll. 3 ff.) and the contemporary "theologian" of the Great Mother, Robert Graves, *The White Goddess: A Historical Grammar of Poetic Myth*, New York, Meridian Books, 1958.

[2] Bronislaw Malinowski, *The Sexual Life of Savages in North-Western Melanesia: An Ethnographic Account of Courtship, Marriage and Family Life Among the Natives of the Trobriand Islands, British New Guinea*, later ed., New York, Schocken Books, n.d., pp. 179 ff.

[3] Bronislaw Malinowski, *The Family among the Australian Aborigines: A Sociological Study*, London, University of London Press, 1913, p. 179.

to feed. The social worker suggested that the lady have a talk with her husband. "Why?" replied the lady. "What does he have to do with it?" An ancient echo of this state of affairs may possibly be recognized in Pliny's teaching concerning the mares of Lusitania, who are inseminated by the west wind.[4]

But the foregoing evidences and others too seldom figure in discussions of the so-called ends of marriage. It seems that while the notion that the male and female should come together for the purpose of procreation is very old in Christianity[5] and has received the approbation of such men as Sigmund Freud,[6] it is nevertheless the case that the urge to mate, to come together, is more deeply situated in the human psyche than any perception of the biological function of that conjunction.

To return to primitive man, we can see that the natural conclusion from his observation of woman would be that it is she who is the productive member of society. It seems not impossible to engage upon a partial reconstruction of man's earliest perceptions of The Way Things Are. The woman is seen as self-reproductive, just as is the earth. Here we may refer to the notion of autochthony to be found, for example, in Plato (*Statesman*, 269b, 271a ff.; *Critias*, 109d, 113c), to which must be conjoined both the notion of man as formed from the soil (as in Gen. 2:7) and its later developments in the image of the potter and the clay (Is. 29:16 and elsewhere). Intimately related to this constellation is the likening of man to the grass or flower of the field (for instance, Job 8:11-19, 15:30-34) and indeed Israel's self-depiction as a vine (Is. 5:1-7) or tree (Jer. 8:13; Rom. 11:17-24) of God's plantation and cultivation, whose "strongest stem" (Ezek. 19:10-14, at 11a) represents the main thrust of growth and hegemony (Is. 11:1).

Again, the woman feeds her young of herself, of her substance; so, too, on a primitive level does Mother Earth, her trees being her breasts. Here we may refer to the fact that the Abraham literature still maintains a certain emphasis upon trees (Gen. 12:6, 13:18, 18:1; cf. 35:4; Deut. 11:30; Josh. 24:26; Judg. 9:37; Is. 1:29-

[4] Pliny, *Natural History*, 8, 67; see also Aristotle, *Historia animalium*, 6, 13 (Crete).

[5] It is found, for example, in the *Clementine Recognitions*, 6, 12.

[6] Sigmund Freud, *Standard Edition of* [*His*] *Complete Psychological Works*, London, Hogarth: Institute of Psychoanalysis, 1963, VI, 316.

30; 57:5), and many of the deviations in ancient Israelite religious practice are centered upon groves (Ezek. 6:13; Hos. 4:13; Jer. 2:20, 3:13; etc.). It should not be necessary to point out that in a pre-agricultural society, man would necessarily be dependent first of all upon edible berries, greens, and nuts (acorns, etc.), at least until such time as he acquired skill at hunting.

Finally, it is instructive to consider that the woman, who is looked upon as the self-reproductive member of society, is subject to a physical cycle roughly corresponding with the cycle of the most changeable aspect of man's celestial experience, the moon. Hence, it is not surprising that the moon is frequently identified with the goddess. But this is not universally true: sometimes the moon is a male, and one might assume that here the moon as god reflects the male meeting the female on her own ground.

Reviewing these attitudes and observations of man in primitive society and the prominent role of woman in that society, it does not seem unnatural, then, that the form of that society's polity should be the matriarchy.

Somewhere along the line, males came to perceive that they too had a role to play, and they have been lording it over the ladies ever since. This perception and much of the resultant takeover seems to have occurred before western man emerged onto the stage of history, properly so called. I say this because some of the pre-historic cave paintings, such as the oft-reproduced Sorcerer of Trois Frères,[7] clearly suggest male self-assertion; again, the Semitic practice of circumcision clearly goes back to the Stone Age, as the flint knives of Joshua 5:2-3 evidence.

Man emerged into history with a fluidity and variety of religious practice that reflect varying stages of self-awareness, especially on the part of the male. I would hypothesize that the notion of the self-reproductive female was first seen to be false by the female herself (perhaps as a result of some separation from the male), who thereupon hit upon the idea of an annual mate who was to be killed before he understood his necessity to the reproductive process: the goddess takes a consort who dies annually; then the goddess and god rule jointly; and then there is only the (male) god.

This problem went full circle; in the Middle Ages, it is not un-

[7] Campbell, *op. cit.*, p. 287.

common to find that the male considered himself the only essential to reproduction and the female provided only a *vas debitum* (suitable vessel) for the growth of the seed. It is indeed fortunate that in those days a daughter never looked like her mother.[8]

The God who manifested himself to Abraham met Abraham on the patriarch's own terms: Abraham would clearly have been unready for the sophisticated monotheism of later times, so Abraham's God did not present himself as the one, only God. And since Abraham was male, El Shaddai[9] may have presented himself as masculine. He may have. And on that basis we perhaps too lightly assume that our God is male.

There is a short, charming letter to God that illustrates how seriously this assumption has been taken by one and all, even today's children. "Dear God, Are boys better than girls. I know you are one but try to be fair. Sylvia." [10]

However, this assumption seems to draw upon such phrases as "Yahweh is a man of war" (Ex. 15:3a) and the attribution to Yahweh of masculine roles over against Israel, as husband (Ezek. 16:8, etc.) and father (Ex. 4:22, etc.). If one is to anthropomorphize the God of Israel, it is possible to understand why it should be done chiefly in terms of the male. But it must not be thought that the maleness of the God of Israel enjoys any particular primacy as an anthropomorphism. Rather, and this is frequently overlooked in too superficial discussions of biblical anthropomorphism, the primary anthropomorphism of the Bible is precisely the notion of the personal God with whom Israel as person (human) may have relations of love, faith, and covenant.[11]

[8] As far as the ancient world is concerned, one might consult Mary Renault's sensitive novelizations of primitive mythology: *The King Must Die*, New York, Pantheon Books, 1958; and *The Bull from the Sea*, New York, Pocket Books, 1963.

[9] El Shaddai, the One of the Mountain, was the one God of Abraham, his shield and friend, but was not necessarily the only God. Thus, assumedly, in Genesis 31:53 the God of Abraham and the God of Nahor, his brother, are not the same, yet they are equally invoked as judges between Jacob and Laban. On the progressive character of Divine Revelation, see, in general, William Foxwell Albright's *From Stone Age to Christianity: Monotheism and Historical Process*, 2nd ed., New York, Doubleday & Company, and Baltimore, Johns Hopkins Press, 1957, Chap. 4, pp. 200-272.

[10] Eric Marshall and Stuart Hample, eds., *Children's Letters to God*, New York, Pocket Books, 1966.

[11] The corollary of this anthropomorphism is the extravagant theomorphism

I say we have too lightly assumed that God is male, because not all the evidence points to the correctness of this assumption. Possibly the most famous of the evidences to the contrary comes from the *Revelations* (or *Shewings*) *of Divine Love* made to Dame Julian (or Jelyan[12]) of Norwich on May 13, 1373. She writes:

> I beheld the working of all the blessed Trinity. In which beholding I saw and understood these three properties: the property of Fatherhood, and the property of Motherhood, and the property of the Lordship—in one God. . . . I saw and understood that the high might of the Trinity is our Father, and the deep wisdome of the Trinity is our Mother, and the great love of the Trinity is our Lord . . . [chap. 58].
>
> And thus is Jesus our true Mother in kind [=nature], of our first making; and he is our true Mother in grace by his taking our made kind. All the fair working and all the sweet kindly offices of most dear Motherhood are appropriated to the second Person [chap. 59].[13]

There is no space here for detailed analyses of Julian's doctrine, but it may not be lightly dismissed as the ravings of a hysterical

---

of Genesis (1:26, etc.): "Then God said, 'Let us make man in our image, after our likeness. . . .'" I shall later allude further to the making of man in God's image. See, too, Martin Buber, *Eclipse of God: Studies in the Relation Between Religion and Philosophy*, New York, Harper & Brothers, 1952, 1957, pp. 14-15.

It is difficult to determine whether Albright means precisely this when he writes: ". . . it cannot be emphasized too strongly that the anthropomorphic conception of Yahweh was absolutely necessary if the God of Israel was to remain a God of the individual Israelite as well as of the people as a whole. . . . For the average worshipper . . . it is very essential that his god be a divinity who can sympathize with his human feelings and emotions, a being whom he can love and fear alternately, and to whom he can transfer the holiest emotions connected with memories of father and mother and friend. In other words, it was precisely the anthropomorphism of Yahweh which was essential to the initial success of Israel's religion" (*op. cit.*, p. 265). This is certainly a valid observation, but it suggests that the success of Israel's religion was calculated!

[12] Thus in the *Book of Margery Kempe*, ed. Sanford Brown Meech, Early English Text Society, Original Series, No. 212, London, Oxford University Press, 1940, p. 42.

[13] *The Revelations of Divine Love of Julian of Norwich*, tr. James Walsh, London, Burns & Oates, 1961. See also Paul Molinari, *Julian of Norwich: The Teaching of a 14th Century English Mystic*, London, Longmans, Green & Co., 1958; S. M. A., "God Is Our Mother," in Cecily Hastings and Donald Nicholl, eds., *Selection 1*, London and New York, Sheed & Ward, 1953, pp. 104-109, reprinted from *Life of the Spirit*, May, 1945, pp. 49-53; David Knowles, *The English Mystical Tradition*, New York, Harper & Row, Publishers, 1961, p. 128.

woman. Listen to a prayer composed by one whom many feel[14] to have been one of the finest theologians—male—of the Middle Ages, Anselm of Canterbury:

> . . . but thou also Jesus, good Lord, art thou not also Mother? Art thou not Mother who art like a hen which gathers her chicks under her wings? Truly, Lord, thou art also Mother. For what others have labored with and have brought forth, they have received from thee. Thou first, for their sake and for those they bring forth, in laboring wert dead, and by dying hast brought forth. . . . Thou, therefore, soul, dead of thyself, run under the wings of Jesus thy Mother and bewail under her feathers thy afflictions. Beg that she heal thy wounds, and that healed, she may restore thee to life. Mother Christ, who gatherest thy chicks under thy wings, this dead chick of thine puts himself under thy wing.[15]

Anselm draws upon Matthew (23:27) for the hen with her brood, which is in itself reminiscent of Old Testament images[16] concerning Yahweh's care for his people; and quite possibly upon the notion that the Church was born from the side of Christ as Eve was born from the side of Adam, an image at least as old as Tertullian.[17]

The motherhood theme is found elsewhere in the Middle Ages,[18] and indeed, centrally, in the Vulgate text of Isaiah (49:1, 15; 66:13), where Israel is said to be the fruit of Yahweh's womb.[19] And earlier in the vision of Saint Perpetua, she experiences Christ as a ewe lamb who is milked.[20] Earlier still, we read in the Christian Odes of Solomon:

[14] E.g., Karl Barth, *Anselm: Fides quaerens intellectum*, tr. Ian W. Robertson, Cleveland and New York, World Publishing Co., 1962.

[15] Anselm of Canterbury, *Oratio ad sanctum Paulum*, in Migne, *PL*, CLVIII, 975-983, at 981-982; and *Opera omnia s. Anselmi*, Edinburgh, Thomas Nelson & Sons, 1946, III, 33-41, at 40-41.

[16] Ex. 19:4; Deut. 32:11; Ruth 2:12; Ps. 17:18, 36:7, 57:1, 61:4, 63:7, 91:4.

[17] Joseph C. Plumpe, *Mater Ecclesia: An Inquiry into the Concept of the Church as Mother in Early Christianity*, Washington, D. C., Catholic University of America Press, 1943, pp. 56 ff.

[18] See André Cabassut, "Une dévotion médiévale peu connue: La dévotion à 'Jésus notre Mère,'" *Revue d'ascétique et de mystique*, XXV (1949), 234-245.

[19] See S. M. A., *op. cit.*, pp. 105-106, where the Douay texts are collected.

[20] See W. H. Shrewing, ed., *The Passion of SS. Perpetua and Felicity, MM.*,

A cup of milk was offered to me;
And I drank it in the sweetness of the delight of the Lord.

The Son is the cup,
And He who is milked is the Father;
And He who milked Him is the Holy Spirit.

Because His breasts were full;
And it was not desireable that His milk should be spilt to no purpose.

And the Holy Spirit opened His [lit., Her] bosom
And mingled the milk of the two breasts of the Father,

And gave the mixture to the world without their knowing:
And they who take [it] are in the fullness of the right hand [19:1-5].[21]

In addition, so that we might see that the imagery of the feminine is applicable to the whole of the Trinity, we may note that the Gospel according to the Hebrews speaks of the Spirit of Yahweh as feminine.[22]

In the Old Testament literature, *Hokma*, Wisdom or Sophia, is Yahweh's pre-existent Beloved, who is sometimes a creature, but in the Septuagint is as well simply *there:* "The Lord possessed me in the beginning of his ways, before he made anything from the beginning" (Prov. 8:22). Christ, according to some,[23] identified himself with this Wisdom. Origen[24] and Justin[25] both appropriate

---

London, Sheed & Ward, 1931, pp. 25-26; more readily accessible is Donald Attwater, *Martyrs: From St. Stephen to John Tung,* New York, Sheed & Ward, 1957, pp. 21-30, at 22-23. The eucharistic depths of this first vision should not remain unplumbed.

The "reversal" of roles, the females being nourished by the substance of the male, finds an interesting parallel in Clare's vision of being nourished at the breast of Francis of Assisi; see Canonization Process, III, 29; *apud* Nesta De Robeck, *St. Clare of Assisi,* Milwaukee, Bruce Publishing Co., 1951.

[21] In J. Rendel Harris and Alphonse Mingana, *The Odes and Psalms of Solomon: Re-edited for the Governors of the John Rylands Library,* 2 vols., London, 1916-1920, II, 298-299; cf. G. Van Moorsel, *The Mysteries of Hermes Trismegistus: A Phenomenologic Study in the Process of Spiritualisation in the Corpus Hermeticum and Latin Asclepius,* Utrecht, 1955, p. 67.

[22] See Jean Daniélou, *The Theology of Jewish Christianity,* Vol. I: *The Development of Christian Doctrine Before the Council of Nicaea,* tr. John A. Baker, London, Darton, Longman & Todd, and Chicago, Henry Regnery Co., 1964, p. 23.

[23] See, e.g., W. D. Davies, *Paul and Rabbinic Judaism: Some Rabbinic Aspects in Pauline Theology,* 2nd ed., London, Society for Promoting Christian Knowledge, 1955, Chap. 7, "The Old and New Torah: Christ the Wisdom of God," pp. 147-176.

[24] Origen, *Commentary on John* 1, 19.

[25] Justin, *Dialogue with Trypho* 41, 1; 100, 4.

Wisdom to the Second Person, while Theophilus of Antioch[26] appropriates it to the Third Person.

Moreover, when we affirm that creation takes place in and through the everlasting Word, we are in fact affirming that this Word is the matrix, the mothering principle, of all things.[27]

The point of all this is not to affirm to you that our God is really a Goddess, but that our God may be spoken of in both masculine and feminine terms. To be anthropomorphic, God may be spoken of as androgynous, in that he possesses and comprehends in an ineffable way all that may be characterized as masculine or feminine. This is true as well of Israel, who is both Yahweh's first-born son[28] and his beloved bride.[29] It is not otherwise with the followers of Jesus: we are the sons of God[30] and the bride of Christ.[31] Further, the human soul, that is, the human being considered as interiority, is both masculine and feminine over against God. It is masculine insofar as, with Jacob/Israel, it contends with God (Gen. 32:24-30; but cf. Job 9:32-35, 13:3 and 15, 19-22, etc., and esp. 38:3). It is feminine in the tradition that would lead to the development of the mystical marriage.[32]

It should be made clear that I am using "androgynous" and "androgyny" not according to the usage of *Webster* (2d ed.) but, with one exception, in a broader and I hope deeper sense than the customary synonyms "hermaphroditic" and "hermaphroditism." "Androgynous" here does not mean "having male and female (physical) characteristics," but "comprising and including both male and

[26] See Daniélou, *op. cit.*, p. 112; see also Irenaeus, *Exposition of the Apostolic Preaching*, 10.

[27] See Aloys Grillmeier, *Christ in Christian Tradition: From the Apostolic Age to Chalcedon (451)*, tr. J. S. Bowden, New York, Sheed & Ward, 1965, pp. 27-35; Oscar Cullmann, *The Christology of the New Testament*, tr. Shirley C. Guthrie and Charles A. M. Hall, London, Student Christian Movement Press, 1959, 1963, pp. 249-269.

[28] See E. J. Foye, "The 'Beloved Son,'" *Front Line*, IV (1965-1966), pp. 129-140.

[29] Jer. 2:2, 3:1 ff.; Ezek. 16; Hos. *passim;* Is. 50:1; etc.

[30] Rom. 8:14-17, 19, 29; 1 Cor. 1:9; 2 Cor. 6:18; Gal. 4:5-9; Heb. 2:10; 12:5-8; Apoc. 21:7.

[31] Eph. 5:21-33; 2 Cor. 11:2; Apoc. 12:1-6, 19:7, 21:2, 22:17.

[32] See *Origen: The Song of Songs: Commentary and Homilies*, tr. R. P. Lawson, Ancient Christian Writers, 26, Westminster, Md., Newman Press, 1957, pp. 29 f. and *passim*. See also note 38, below.

female." In this usage, the human race is androgynous, as is each member of it; and this, in contrast with the exceptional character of formal hermaphroditism.

To return to the matter at hand, it is not unusual, in interpretations that predate the documentary approach to the composition of Genesis, to find that Adam himself was androgynous, or hermaphroditic, until Eve was separated from him.[33] It seems that Karl Stern[34] crows at false dawn in citing Genesis and Plato's *Symposium* in the matter of the original androgyny: "It is remarkable that here for once, before the Christian epoch, Greek and Jew agree"; for Professor Stern has not read his Grecian source as closely as he might have. Aristophanes' speech puts forth three dyads: male-male, male-female, and female-female; and in this speech, the highest form of *restitutio* is between male and male, while the lowest is between male and female, a proposition to which someone in the Genesis tradition could not readily assent.[35] Both the Priestly and Yahwist sources affirm the androgyny of mankind: male and female. It is the Yahwist source that provides us with that glorious exultation in human androgyny in Genesis 2:23-24; and in fact, it may be that the Priestly source understands mankind's androgyny as his special mode of being the image of God, for it is twice said, ". . . in the image of God he created him, male and female he created them" (1:27; see 5:1-2). This by no means exhausts the meaning of man as the image of God.[36] There is another aspect of man as image which I had perceived, and to which I have already alluded, and had presented in my class lectures with a certain diffidence—because I thought that I had "made it up." I have since abandoned my diffidence, since I have found the point very well made in the *Clementine Recognitions* (5, 23): "If you really wish to worship the image of God, you would do good to man, and so worship the true image of God in him."

But to return to the image of God as male and female, it should be said that just as God is the source of all the apparent contraries

[33] See, e.g., Davies, *op. cit.*, pp. 48-55; I have been unable to verify Professor Davies' reference to the *Jewish Encyclopedia* on p. 48.

[34] Karl Stern, *The Flight from Woman*, New York, Farrar, Straus & Giroux, 1965, p. 11.

[35] The Stephanus reference is *Symposium*, 189d-193d; but cf. 177e.

[36] See above, note 11, and corresponding text.

of creation, and just as all things are one in him and will be one in him who is the composition of all opposition, so, too, the male and female, as the poles of the one humanity, show forth in their one-ing the one-ing of all things that is yet to be universally perceived.[37]

I understand from friends who know about such things as biology that every human being is androgynous, that is, contains the masculine and feminine physiologically. This seems to be even more true on the psychic level. On a very obvious plane: When I speak, I emit the word; I sow the seed. When I listen, I receive the word; I am the receptacle of the seed. In Philo it is the feminine virtue that plays the masculine role by fecundating the mind.[38]

Jung, as you know, believes that the unconscious of every male is female, and vice versa.[39] I do not want to dismiss Jung, or on the other hand to propound his anima-animus theory, though I must confess that I am apprehensive of what can only be called his Gnosticism.[40] But it must be said that he has furnished us with many valuable insights, as attested by Josef Goldbrunner[41] and Raymond Hostie,[42] and further, that he has furnished us with many occasions for the rethinking of basic notions.[43] But in regard to his anima-animus theory, which I do not have the clinical competence to judge, I would note that there is a fragmentation within the human psyche, what Augustine calls a *distentio animae*,[44] a

[37] See E. J. Foye, "'You Shall Indeed Share My Cup'—Mt. 20:23," *Front Line*, Summer, 1964, p. 33.

[38] Philo, *On Abraham*, 101, and *On Flight and Finding*, 51 f.; see also Sidney G. Sowers, *The Hermeneutics of Philo and Hebrews*, Richmond, John Knox Press, 1965, p. 135.

[39] See esp. Carl G. Jung, *Mysterium Coniunctionis: An Inquiry into the Separation of Psychic Opposites in Alchemy*, tr. R. F. C. Hull, Bollingen Series, The Collected Works of C. G. Jung, 14, New York, Pantheon Books, 1963.

[40] Buber, *op. cit.*, pp. 136-137; Maurice S. Friedman, *Martin Buber: The Life of Dialogue*, Chicago, University of Chicago Press, 1955, Index, "Gnosticism."

[41] Joseph Goldbrunner, *Individuation: A Study of the Depth Psychology of Carl Gustav Jung*, New York, Pantheon Books, 1956.

[42] Raymond Hostie, *Religion and the Psychology of Jung*, tr. G. R. Lamb, New York, Sheed & Ward, 1957.

[43] Here one has only to advert to the breadth of the subject matter in and the eminence of the contributors to the *Eranos Jahrbücher;* see the series Papers from the Eranos Yearbook, ed. Joseph Campbell, Bollingen Series, New York, Pantheon Books, 1954 *et seq*.

[44] Augustine, *Confessions*, 11, 29; see Jean Guitton, *Le Temps et l'éternité chez Plotin et saint Augustin*, Paris, Boivin & Cie., 1933, 1955, pp. 192-193.

diaspora of the soul,[45] which calls for a one-ing, an *intentio*, a unification, which in Christian terms is accomplished by infused charity, effecting the perfecting, the maturation of the person in Christ. To use Julian's trinitarian terminology, the fatherhood and the motherhood in a man must be oned before the lordship in man can be made manifest.

Again, it is essential that each person fully accept the human race as androgynous and make peace with the other sex, for this androgyny is a gift of God and may not be despised. Karl Barth suggests that should a person consciously choose a vocation calculated to prevent contact with the other sex, that person is in sin.[46] I will not concur with Barth, but I will say that that person will not be sanctified within that vocation until the motivation is changed.

In a very interesting survey article entitled "Why I Am a Sister," [47] wherein a variety of women discuss their motivations with regard to their vocations, a persistent acknowledgment is found that many a woman had to change her motivation—she had entered for the wrong reasons—in order to persist in her vocation.

I do not wish to imply that these wrong reasons necessarily had to do with rejection of the sexual other, or that men and women do not enter other vocations, such as marriage, for the wrong reasons. I merely wish to point out that one can be doing the right thing for the wrong reason and that the wrong reason cannot provide one with sustenance. We may here refer to an exchange of some vintage, that between Gerald Vann and John C. Ford.[48]

Our seminary system, which is meant to produce the elders of our community, our presbyterate, frequently discourages contact with the sexual other, with the feminine. That this is the case should not require serious documentation. One may refer, for example, to the recent hue and cry in Italy concerning a book which ex-

[45] This interpretation of Augustine's meaning is from Gilles Quispel, "Time and History in Patristic Thought," in *Man and Time*, Papers from the Eranos Yearbook, 3, Bollingen Series, New York, Pantheon Books, 1957, pp. 85-107, at 106.

[46] See Karl Barth, *Church Dogmatics*, vol. III: *The Doctrine of Creation*, Part II, tr. H. Knight *et al.*, Edinburgh, T. & T. Clark, 1960, pp. 290 ff.

[47] *Jubilee*, October, 1964, pp. 10-21.

[48] Gerald Vann, "Unconscious Motivation and Pseudo-Virtue," and John C. Ford, "Reply to Father Vann," *Homiletic and Pastoral Review*, November, 1956, pp. 115-123 and 124-127.

pressed the opinion that current seminary practice and ideology with regard to the feminine was not leading to a great deal of maturity on the part of the seminary's alumni.[49]

The seminary situation in the United States is not quite as bad as it seems to be in Italy; but it is not that good, particularly in the matter under discussion. For example, a recent book edited by James Keller and Richard Armstrong, *Apostolic Renewal in the Seminary: In the Light of Vatican Council II* (1965), nowhere adverts to the matter; indeed, the one chapter that should handle it, "Spiritual Growth and Apostolic Formation in the Seminary" by Edmund E. Veillesse (pp. 75-88), sidesteps the question by suggesting that seminarians tend to be less mature than their counterparts in the university or in married life because they do not have the "*real responsibilities*" (p. 83) their counterparts do.

This type of isolation from and discouragement of contacts with the feminine does the elderhood a profound disservice. One of the major means to maturation available to human beings is precisely contact with the sexual other. And this observation is more applicable to men than to women. I recently came across a study of the relationship between life adjustment and marital status. The most adjusted members of the human race, according to this sampling, are married men. The least adjusted are the unmarried men.[50] It is not my conclusion that all men should be married; on the other hand, I will not concede for a moment that all who are unmarried under the present system of mandatory celibacy should be unmarried. While I know, and have known, celibates who have achieved an astonishing depth as human beings, I would suggest that they have achieved this depth having made their peace with the sexual other, and despite their marital status.

. . .

But I can cite a letter from a distinguished theologian, Bernard Häring, in the pages of the *National Catholic Reporter* (July 20, 1966, p. 4).

While I would challenge Father Häring's scriptural interpreta-

[49] *National Catholic Reporter*, January 11, 1967, p. 6.

[50] See Genevieve Knupfer, Walter Clark, and Robin Room, "The Mental Health of the Unmarried," *American Journal of Psychiatry*, February, 1966, pp. 841-851.

tions as being seriously defective, I should like here to concentrate upon an attitude he projects. He writes:

> John Leo's article . . . is an invitation, one might imagine, to older girls who have not been able to find husbands and to a few frustrated nuns "to question the relevance of the isolation and caste life imposed by celibacy." . . . The senseless discussions on celibacy have caused great confusion. Girls have approached irreproachable priests and expressed their hope that the Church would allow them to get married. An innocent friendliness on the part of good priests was misunderstood as a first step on which the Church would liberate him from "enforced celibacy."

I would suggest that we have here a rather subtle exposure of the blatant male ego (which I share), wherein the celibate tells himself that of course all these women are after him; and he could have them, any and all of them, but for his sacred vow (which is not of course a vow). And he will never know that his euphoric self-aggrandizement is utter nonsense unless he decides to break his sacred vow and try to seduce all these women.

I would further suggest that there is nothing more salubrious for a man's ego than a wife who both loves him and—for better or for worse—knows him. I do conclude that it can be dangerous not to heed the counsel of the word of God to be found in the Book of Sirach: "Do not deprive yourself of a wise and good wife, for her charm is worth more than gold" (7:19).

Just as rejection of the sexual other can prove to be a disaster, whether we speak in terms of mental health or Christian perfection, so, too, when we speak of the Church, the community of the people of God, we perceive this same danger. The Church's authenticity as the Living Word of God upon this earth is seriously impaired when there is a rejection of the feminine or the masculine or both.

Does not Paul reject the male-female distinction himself in his letter to the Galatians? He writes: ". . . for in Jesus Christ you are all sons of God, through faith. For as many of you as were baptized into Christ have put on Christ. There is neither Jew nor Greek, there is neither slave nor free, there is neither male nor female; for you are all one in Christ Jesus" (3:26-28; see Col. 1:20, 3:11). Jesus the Messiah who has oned all things in himself has abolished all grounds for distinction among men; Paul is not denying that male and female do exist but asserting that, as all are one and equal before God, Christians are all equally possessors of the spirit of Sonship: they are equally Christ.

One cannot be very impressed by the claims sometimes made in favor of Christianity's assertion of the dignity of womankind, for if the assertion was in fact made, it seems to have caused little difference in Christian society. However, the egalitarian movements of the last few centuries which have resulted in the increasing emancipation of women have been Christian in spirit or goal, if not in leadership.

Paul—doubtless under the influence of the social fabric of his era and Jewish synagogue practice—seems at times unwilling to follow the logic of his doctrine: "I permit no woman to teach or to have authority over men; she is to keep silent" (1 Tim. 2:12). Again, "It is shameful for a woman to speak in church" (1 Cor. 14:35b).

It will be noted that Paul's doctrine of men praying uncovered and women covered is just the opposite of what is done in the "normative" Judaism of our present-day experience. But this fact may not be taken to mean that Paul's practice is not drawn from Jewish custom, for Jewish usage at that time was far more diverse than, for example, present-day Judaism's normative heritage would lead us to believe. A striking example of diversity is to be found in the "scandalous" synagogue at Dura-Europa.[51]

But Paul, in his command against women's speaking in church, is inconsistent in his inconsistency. For he does recognize that a woman might speak in church, since he says earlier, ". . . any woman who prays or prophesies with her head unveiled dishonors her head" (1 Cor. 11:5); and it is clear from the context that this prophetic activity takes place in church as part of the liturgy (see 14:13-33). Moreover, we know very well that the Spirit of prophecy does not restrict his activities to the male: thus, the daughters of Philip the Evangelist are spoken of as being prophetesses (Acts 21:9), Miriam was a prophetess (Ex. 15:20; see Num.

[51] See Erwin R. Goodenough, *Jewish Symbols in the Greco-Roman Period*, 12 vols., New York, Pantheon Books, 1953 *et seq.*, vol. XI.

12:2), as was Deborah (Judg. 4:4), Huldah (2 Kings 22:14), Noadiah (Neh. 6:14), and she who was possibly wife to Isaiah (8:3); so, too, in New Testament times was Anna (Lk. 2:36). Indeed, the promise made through Joel specifically includes women as true speakers of God's word: "And it shall come to pass afterward, that I will pour out my spirit in all flesh; your sons and daughters shall prophesy" (2:28 [Mt. 3:1]; cf. Acts 2:17). Consequently, it is difficult in the extreme to maintain an exclusion of women from full participation in church affairs on the basis of an inconsistent and possibly dubious application of a doctrinal principle.

Too often, it may be observed, Paul's "neither male nor female" is taken to be a rejection of sexuality itself in favor of a make-believe angelism. I do not refer here to sexual abstinence but, more fundamentally, to a denial of the fact that one is irrevocably a part of an androgynous humankind, wherein one is necessarily male or female over against others who are necessarily either male or female. In this denial, one tries to pretend that one is something that God never made.

This "unnaturalism," which I think does not require critical description here, is not only found in the individual's conception of his or her own calling, but has managed to encroach upon the devotional life of the Church and even upon its doctrinal self-understanding. I do not mean to say that the Church ever formally proposed angelism, but in its practice it has rejected the feminine; and this rejection has inevitably entailed the rejection or at least the caricature of the masculine.

It will be agreed that our medieval and early modern periods may be characterized as rejecting or suppressing the female in both society in general and the Church in particular. Within this context, if a woman wanted to dedicate herself to God—indeed, to do anything at all in such a society—she had to confirm this rejection in herself by dressing in widow's weeds and becoming cloistered, thus making herself both sexually and humanly inaccessible. It was as though womankind were being punished because mankind was sexual, and sex was dirty. This is a part of what one can only call Augustine's obscene purity in *The City of God*, 14, 23-24; one need not comment here upon Augustine's apparent heartlessness in his rejection of his always nameless concubine, but rather one can point to an equally heartless rejection *within* Christian marriage that earned the praise (!) of Gregory the Great.[52]

In the rejection of the feminine, the sanctuary did not become thereby more masculine; rather, it lost the balance that the presence of the feminine gives to the masculine, and took on all too frequently the lisp of fawning servility. And generally speaking, there were no men in the nave—just women, children, and old people; for most men tended to reject the connotation of inferiority that "layman" as a term came to have, and to be repelled by the notion of not having a voice in their own affairs. Apart from our present usage of "lay" as an equivalent of incompetence, we may consider the evidence collected in the Oxford English Dictionary under "lewd." About 890, "lewd" meant "lay" or "layman." Thus one might speak of lewd freres: lay brothers. Later one might speak of the learned and the lewd, that is, scholar and nonscholar, just as today we speak of a book's being written for both scholars and laymen. Our present-day use of "lewd" as "libidinous" was well developed long before the end of the Middle Ages.

At any rate, while there remained men and women in the Church, we may say that there were men in the sanctuary and there were women in the nave, but that the relations between them were so unnatural as to present a caricature of true humanity. It is still the tradition in the Latin churches that men, if they are interested in the Church, become ecclesiastics; but a man does not go to church—that is something women do.[53]

During this period as well, we find the devotional life of the Church becoming feminine in the worst sense of the word. That the following developments are due to more factors than the rejection of the feminine can hardly be doubted; the battle against Arianism would have to be factored into any final explanation of the rise of the devotion to the Crucified, for example.[54] All I am asserting here is

[52] See Gregory the Great, *Dialogues*, 4, 12.

[53] But attitudes like this should not be thought to be restricted to Mediterranean countries. James Joyce's *Ulysses*, for example, has as one of its deep-running themes Stephen's refusal to kneel at his dying mother's bedside, or, in churchly translation, to bend the knee before ecclesiastical authoritarian claims. His whole attitude seems capable of epitome thus: I am a man; I do not grovel before other men.

[54] See Joseph A. Jungmann, *Pastoral Liturgy*, New York, Herder and Herder, 1962, pp. 1-101.

that the rejection of the feminine ought to be considered as a major reason for the popularity of these devotions.

Having been rejected by society and the Church, the woman found her consolation in devotions wherein it was the woman and not man who was central or at least meaningful. A psychologist might speak of this as sublimation. The Madonna comes immediately to mind: she as feminine is central, and her role necessarily involves the helplessness of the male in the form of the *bambino*. Or again, it will be remembered that during the Middle Ages, devotion to the crucifix or to the *Pietà* was especially popular, once again involving the helpless male. It may not be suggested, as I have said above, that the masculine rejection of the female directly caused the rise of devotion to the Crucified; but the popularity of this devotion may indicate the woman's unconscious rejection of the pretensions of the male. Further, it may not be without significance that the centrality of the mystery of the Resurrection, the exaltation of the male and indeed of humanity itself, is particularly obscured at this time. With this obscuration went the full import of the Resurrection: that salvation has been accomplished, that sin has been conquered. Anyone who has listened closely to the prayers of our present liturgy knows very well that we do not pray as though we really believe we are redeemed; the heart of the message has been seriously beclouded.[55] Indeed, we may say that when one essential element of humanity is rejected, the whole is rejected; the hope for one dies in the abyss of the failure of the other.

We are an androgynous people. God has created us male and female. If we are to express ourselves as a truly human community, we must do so androgynously. If we reduce the feminine to silence, we are rejecting ourselves and defining in advance the graces God may give and to whom he may give them. If we allow the feminine full voice in the Church, then we must allow her her rightful place in the councils of leadership, in the elderhood[56] of the Church. When we ask whether women are ordainable in the Church, we are

[55] See, in general, F. X. Durrwell, *The Resurrection: A Biblical Study*, tr. Rosemary Sheed, New York, Sheed & Ward, 1960.

[56] On the elderhood, see my preliminary studies "The People of God and Their Work," in Frederick R. McManus, ed., *The Revival of the Liturgy*, New York, Herder and Herder, 1963, pp. 114-124; and "Rome and the Episcopacy," *Front Line*, II (1963-1964), 82-96. It is my hope that a fuller study of these matters may soon be among my possibilities.

in fact asking two questions: first, whether woman, any woman, is capable of maturity, of the fullness of humanity (and I do not savor the position of a man who would answer that question negatively); and second, whether we are ready finally to allow the Spirit of God to breathe where it will (Jn. 3:8), or will continue to quench the Spirit (1 Thess. 5:19).

VI Religious Secularity

For all things are yours, whether Paul, or Apollos, or Cephas; or the world, or life, or death; or things present, or things to come—all are yours, and you are Christ's, and Christ is God's.

I CORINTHIANS 3:22-23

REV. JAMES J. MEGIVERN, C.M.

16 A Theology of Incarnationalism

The whole fabric of Christian theology is woven between an *even now* and a *not yet*. The richness of the biblical revelation is such that a wealth of material is readily accessible to build an impressive structure about either of these terms. But since both are adverbial, concerning time, it is obvious that any theology of history is highly problematical until they are somehow harmoniously integrated. If one puts the accent on the *even now*, it is the Incarnation, the first coming of Christ, and its effects that are highlighted; if the focus is trained on the *not yet*, it is the parousia, the second coming of Christ, that is stressed. These two views, the incarnational and the eschatological, can never be allowed to ignore one another, for each is incomplete, each is partial, each is true.

By the same token, each is susceptible of particular temptations. The incarnational can foster a naive optimism that forgets the reality of sin in the Church, giving rise to all kinds of triumphalism, canonizing the status quo, resisting all talk of reform. The eschatological can induce a kind of pessimism which finds it difficult to take this life and its tasks and achievements very seriously, and which can lead to the pie-in-the-sky outlook that languishes in this vale of tears. The pros and cons, the strengths and weaknesses, and the chief proponents of each tendency in recent theological writing are readily available in Martin D'Arcy's *The Meaning and Matter of History*, Peter Riga's *Catholic Thought in Crisis*, and

James Connolly's *Human History and the Word of God*,[1] to mention but three.

However, it seems to me that the long-standing tension of the incarnational and eschatological viewpoints has entered a new phase in the past few years. The Second Vatican Council certainly played a role here, but so did a number of other factors. I refer to the all-pervasive contemporary interest in the *secular*. Within a matter of months, the bookstands sported Harvey Cox's *Secular City*, Bernard Meland's *Secularization of Modern Culture*, Colin Williams' *Faith in a Secular Age*, Eric Mascall's *Secularization of Christianity*, Larry Shiner's *Secularization of History*, and Ronald Gregor Smith's *Secular Christianity*.[2]

One immediate consequence of this sudden deluge of material on secularity is the likelihood of a lessening of attention to the eschatological. It is the world of the here and now that has the spotlight. This naturally gives an additional advantage to incarnationalism, providing even a sense of urgency that is impatient of any further hesitation. The spirit of the day is one of action, of engagement in every program that promises to improve the condition of man; and the Christian who thinks twice about taking his stand in the midst of this movement had best realize that he is thereby stamped "irrelevant" and passed by.

And yet, the pressure of the times is no excuse for the Christian to jettison his theology. On the contrary, it is especially in such an era of major transition as our own that every aspect of change must be subjected to close criticism. This is the prophetic function of theology, far different from an attitude of immobilism that protests the *fact* of change without concern for either the starting point or the term. Granting the absolute necessity and thus de-

[1] Martin D'Arcy, *The Meaning and Matter of History*, New York, Meridian Books, 1961; Peter Riga, *Catholic Thought in Crisis*, Milwaukee, Bruce Publishing Co., 1963; James Connolly, *Human History and the Word of God*, New York, Macmillan Company, 1965.

[2] Harvey Cox, *Secular City*, New York, Macmillan Company, 1965; Bernard Meland, *The Secularization of Modern Cultures*, New York, Oxford University Press, 1966; Colin Williams, *Faith in a Secular Age*, New York, Harper & Row, Publishers, 1966; Eric Mascall, *The Secularization of Christianity*, New York, Holt, Rinehart & Winston, 1965; Larry Shiner, *The Secularization of History: An Introduction of the Theology of Friedrich Gogarten*, Nashville, Abingdon Press, 1966; Ronald Gregor Smith, *Secular Christianity*, New York, Harper & Row, Publishers, 1966.

sirability of change, theology must then fill the role discerning the how and the why in each instance.

So much ink has flowed recently about secularity that it is highly questionable whether any good purpose can be served by taking up the topic again. Yet, in view of our concern with incarnationalism, perhaps it will be worthwhile attempting to single out a few strains that bear on this.

First of all, the very word *world* is highly ambiguous, and it is the New Testament itself that is largely responsible for this. In its simplest sense, it designates merely the whole of created reality, that which was made by the Logos; this in turn can be narrowed down at times to human reality, the world of peoples. This is the world into which the Logos came, the world so loved by God that He gave it His only Son. But third, "the world" very often means humanity as sinful, as rebellious against God and thus deserving of judgment. This and the first meaning are combined in the very same verse in Saint John's Prologue: the world (created reality) was made by Him, yet the world (sinful humanity) knew Him not. The same two meanings have to be invoked if we are to make much sense out of the saying about being *in* the world but not *of* it.[3]

In the light of this plurality of senses in Scripture itself, it is worth suggesting that perhaps a certain ambivalence is essential for a Christian, a willingness to say yes *and* no to the whole question of the secular, demanding that the precise sense be first determined in each instance. Admittedly, it is much easier to adopt a simple black-and-white position, as Brent Bozell does in this quotation:

> Christ put Himself in stark, uncompromising opposition to the ways of the world. He taught men to turn to Him, away from the world, or be damned. He taught nothing else. . . . The Christian who urges the Church to come to terms with *this* world, with *this* age, is either a victim of despair, or has ceased to be a Christian at all.[4]

It may be convenient to be able to sum up one's position so tidily, but it has the slight disadvantage of ignoring a large part of the

[3] See Christopher Senft, "World," in J. J. von Allmen, ed., *Vocabulary of the Bible*, tr. P. J. Allcock *et al.*, London, Lutterworth Press, 1958, pp. 469-471.

[4] Brent Bozell, in *National Catholic Reporter*, March 22, 1967, p. 6.

New Testament, as well as Vatican II, which did not blush to say, for example, "[The Catholic Church] is convinced that she can be abundantly and variously helped by the world in the matter of preparing the ground for the Gospel." [5]

But perhaps it is the opposite extreme that is the greater temptation today. The attitude of uncompromising hostility to the world summed up by Bozell was an attitude of other days, but has little appeal to the postconciliar Catholic who has come into touch with the thought and spirit of men like Teilhard de Chardin and Karl Rahner, not to mention Pope John XXIII. Most educated Catholics are more likely today to be embarrassed by such hostility, apologizing for past expressions of it on the part of the Church and growing impatient with its lingering manifestations in ultraconservative areas. Hence, by our very recognition that the pendulum is now in full swing in the other direction, honesty itself and fidelity to revelation require our attempt to see what danger of distortion we are most prone to in this situation.

Upon becoming aware of the shortcomings of the recent past, especially the omnipresent triumphalism in our thinking about the Church, we tend by psychological reaction simply to transfer those same attitudes to the secular. One can easily fall into celebrating the secular city with all the triumphalism that ever infected the Church. This is, it hardly needs saying, unreasonable. We should be at least as willing and ready to criticize defective aspects of the world as we are to criticize those of the Church! In other words, while recognizing the need to find the proper language for communicating the Gospel to modern man, we must not confuse communication with accommodation, which would put to one side the role of the cross.[6]

One of the risks that secularity thus poses for the incarnationalist

[5] *Constitution on the Church in the Modern World*, sec. 40. The explicit awareness of the various biblical senses can be seen in section 2 of the same document. As Cardinal Montini, the present Pope, spoke in terms quite unlike Bozell's: "We must love our times, our civilization, our technology, our art, our sport, our world. We must love while trying to understand, to sympathize, to esteem, to serve, to suffer. We must love with the heart of Christ and the plenitude of God" (quoted in Msgr. Gerard Philips, *Achieving Christian Maturity*, Chicago, Franciscan Herald Press, 1966, p. 95).

[6] See Gabriel Fackre, "The Issue of Transcendence in the New Theology," in Martin Marty and Dean Peerman, eds., *New Theology No. 4*, New York, Macmillan Company, 1967, p. 181.

is a too facile identification of the Church with the world, or at least of the Church's work with human progress. There is a sense in which the Church *is* the world: the first biblical sense, the world as all creation, of which the Church is part.[7] But the recovery of this awareness, and the advantages it brings for overcoming past misconceptions, would cause greater harm than good if the result were an obscuring of the Church's proper task. It is especially in trying to evaluate the contribution of Teilhard de Chardin that this problem must be kept in mind. As Christopher Mooney says, "Teilhard's great originality here is his insistence that the salvific action of God is also to be found at work in the natural energies of man, and, conversely, that the natural evolutionary process does not operate and above all cannot reach its own natural fulfillment independently of Christ." [8] The necessary caveat to this evolutionary approach is well voiced by Karl Rahner: "Christianity knows no history which would evolve of its own inner power into the kingdom of God itself, and it does not really matter whether one conceives this kingdom as the realm of the enlightened mind, or of the fully civilized man, or of the classless society or in any other way whatsoever." [9]

Another way to express this whole issue is to distinguish civilization from evangelization clearly. Christians certainly have a major role to perform in the former, but the latter cannot be confused with it or forgotten. Evangelization presupposes civilization but has its own inherent demands.[10]

What we are saying in effect is that secularization in itself is a neutral process. True, "It is always a threat to historic religions, but it can be the ferment that cleanses the inward parts." [11] This positive function of secularization is a prominent feature in the theology of Friedrich Gogarten, who is being more and more recognized as

[7] See J. B. Metz, "The Church and the World," in T. Patrick Burke, ed., *The Word in History*, Saint Xavier Symposium, New York, Sheed & Ward, 1966, p. 81.

[8] Christopher F. Mooney, S.J., *Teilhard de Chardin and the Mystery of Christ*, New York, Harper & Row, Publishers, 1966, p. 206.

[9] Karl Rahner, *Theological Investigations*, vol. IV: *More Recent Writings*, Baltimore, Helicon Press, 1967, Chap. 5, "History of the World and Salvation-History," p. 111.

[10] The expression is from Alec Vidler, *Christian Belief and This World*, New York, Seabury Press, 1957, p. 44; cited in Connolly, *op. cit.*, p. 146.

[11] Meland, *op. cit.*, p. 163.

quite as much a pioneer in this matter as Dietrich Bonhoeffer. The interesting and disputed point is the contention that the Christian gospel itself is the *source* of secularization, because it frees man from the world, "de-divinizing" the world, placing it in the power of man;[12] in fact, it has been called the task of the Church to keep the world secular,[13] not to let it take on divine aspects that do not belong to it. Indeed, it is difficult to substantiate such a claim historically, especially when we see that Bonhoeffer himself dates the origin of the process back to the thirteenth century,[14] while Gogarten gives the credit to Martin Luther's emphasis on justification by faith alone in the sixteenth century.[15] But it must be admitted that it makes a lot of sense theologically. Let us pursue it a little further.

Arend Van Leeuwen makes much of the fact that "technological revolution was nurtured in the bosom of Christian civilization and indeed is one of its 'children.' "[16] Modern science was made possible by the doctrine of creation, which desacralizes nature, enabling one to treat it objectively. One area where this has an impact is that of church structures, or for that matter, any social structures. The *ontocratic* order is being replaced by the *technocratic.*

In the ontocratic order, all structures were sacralized; the status quo was canonized by the presumption that what existed in time reflected the eternal. This order was shattered first by the *theocratic* in the Judeo-Christian revelation, where the rule of God over all undercuts any sacral order and allows for the Lord to break open any inhibiting structures to let a new mode of existence emerge.[17] This in turn paved the way for the technocratic, where man assumes his God-given responsibility, applying his ingenuity to find techniques to bring the world to serve the needs of humanity. In Marcel's phrase, "Man now runs his own life."[18]

[12] See Smith, *op. cit.*, pp. 150 ff.
[13] See Shiner, *op. cit.*, p. 173.
[14] Smith, *op. cit.*, p. 178.
[15] See, e.g., Van A. Harvey, *The Historian and the Believer,* New York, Macmillan Company, 1966, p. 135.
[16] Arend T. Van Leeuwen, *Christianity in World History: The Meeting of Faiths of East and West,* New York, Charles Scribner's Sons, 1964, p. 403.
[17] See Richard Shaull, "Christian Mission in a Technological Era," *Cross Currents,* Fall, 1965, p. 462.
[18] Quoted in Smith, *op. cit.*, p. 169.

Such a picture of man "come of age" is still in itself neither curse nor boon, but an acceptance of man's changed position resulting from technology. There is no need "to write God's obituary in order to affirm humanity" [19] in its altered stance. But this is a mammoth challenge for the institutional side of the Church. An ontocratic order as in the past (since Constantine?) was a much more secure kind of existence, one that allowed the Church to propose programs of action and codes of canon law for whole continents and entire generations, confident of their basic validity and applicability. But in the technocratic order, such stability is gone; in a perpetually changing world, one cannot reasonably act as if nothing is changing and expect to be taken seriously. In a truly incarnational approach, every change that affects the life of modern man is the proper object of intense scrutiny, with consequences for much of Church activity.

At this point, we must move on to see just what kind of position Vatican II took in the realm of secularity. It is now acknowledged that in at least one of its earlier stages Schema 13, on the Church and the modern world, reflected an uncritical acceptance of the thought of Teilhard de Chardin. The identification of technological progress with Christological progress was rather complete.[20] This tendency was understandable enough as an effort to make up for the opposite mistake in the past. But fortunately, the repeated revisions of the schema in the light of the criticisms leveled against it by various Council Fathers resulted in an end product that is finely nuanced and can certainly stand as a guide for some time to come. Almost all the elements of dispute between the incarnational and eschatological approaches over the past decade are brought together in sections 33-39, and a valiant effort is made to do them all justice. It is surely safe to say that any progress toward a solution will have to take these paragraphs as its starting point. Little more than that can be said. This is one of the classical instances of a council at its best, recognizing the difference between faith and theology. It rules out a number of unacceptable positions; it asserts the biblical elements that must figure in any solution; it gives a general

[19] Fackre, *op. cit.*, p. 183.

[20] Joseph Ratzinger, *Theological Highlights of Vatican II*, Glen Rock, N. J., Paulist Press, 1966, p. 159.

orientation; then it leaves the question *open* as to the precise relation between spiritual and temporal activity in human life.[21]

Indeed, one of the most heartening characteristics of this entire document is its recognition of modern complexity, its refusal to give pat answers to complicated questions. One of the most complicated is certainly this one, which it calls man's "total" or "integral" vocation. It is one and the same human person who is called both to seek the Kingdom of God and to build the city of man, and to exclude or ignore either is to demonstrate that one does not know the meaning of man. This holds just as true for man "come of age" as for man in any other era of his history, but his changed relationship to the world makes the proper harmonization of these two aspects more problematical than ever.

In some sections of the *Constitution on the Church in the Modern World*—for example, section 4—one can sense an awareness of the growing complexity of man's relation to and position in the world, and is reminded of the analysis of existential psychology in the terms made current by Ludwig Binswanger: the *Umwelt*, the *Mitwelt*, and the *Eigenwelt*. The *Umwelt* refers to the world of objects, and it is over this that modern man is more and more winning mastery. The *Mitwelt* is the world of interrelationships with other men, and judging from the tragedy of Vietnam and the like, modern man has made no progress whatsoever except in the extent and the intensity of the expression of his savagery. The *Eigenwelt* is man's self-world in which he meets, faces up to, and lives with himself, and in some ways this today is the greatest problem of all.[22] Technology has had a vastly different impact on each of these three worlds. In giving man greater mastery over his *Umwelt*, it creates greater dangers for his *Mitwelt*, and can create utter chaos in his *Eigenwelt* by anxiety, dehumanization, and frustration of ideals. These three modalities of the modern world allow one to make a more sophisti-

[21] See R. A. Sigmond, O.P., "A History of the Pastoral Constitution on the Church in the Modern World: II," *IDO-C Bulletin*, no. 66-3, p. 4.

[22] See Ludwig Binswanger's contributions in Rollo May, Ernest Angel, and Henri P. Ellenberger, eds., *Existence: A New Dimension in Psychiatry and Psychology*, New York, Basic Books, 1958; cited in Walter Ong, S.J., *In the Human Grain: Technological Culture and Its Effect on Man, Literature, and Religion*, New York, Macmillan Company, 1967, pp. 133 ff.

cated evaluation of the whole question of secularity, avoiding both extremes of naive optimism and myopic pessimism.

While it does not crystallize the precise relationship between the two aspects of man's integral vocation, the Council does indicate clearly where the answer is to be sought. The *Incarnation* is invoked in every section. To reverse a saying of George Webber, to take the world seriously is to take the Incarnation seriously.[23] The section on the meaning of man ends up with Christ, the New Man, the second Adam; the treatment of human community is crowned with the solidarity of the divine Word incarnate with men; the discussion of human activity in history is rounded off with the paschal mystery, the work of Christ; and the conclusion of the whole presents Him Who is alpha and omega. Even stylistically, the point could hardly be driven home more forcefully. The Church has no other answer to any of man's questions but the unique Word spoken by the Father and born of the Virgin Mary.

To say this, however, can end up being rather embarrassing to the incarnationalist. This, the Incarnation, is the central truth of the Christian faith, the heart of the gospel; and yet in our day, there is a swelling chorus of voices daring to point out that, of all things, our *Christology* is underdeveloped.[24] Teilhard de Chardin once wrote that "Christology, in contrast to Mariology, has made practically no progress at all in recent centuries." [25] Along with this recognition, however, is the parallel awareness that the area that needs development is not so much the *ad intra*, Christ in Himself—His consciousness, duality of natures, and so forth. This aspect has had the benefit of most of the attention in Christian tradition. What calls for fuller treatment is the *ad extra*, the relation of Christ to the world. In this sense, our greatest contemporary need is a truly *"secular" Christology*. Christ's primacy over the universe, His central role in the creation and redemption of the cosmos as sketched in *Ephesians* and *Colossians*, has never really been taken very seri-

[23] See George W. Webber, "The Christian Minister and the Social Problems of the Day," in Martin Marty and Dean Peerman, eds., *New Theology No. 3*, New York, Macmillan Company, 1966, p. 159.

[24] See Helmut Riedlinger, "How Universal Is Christ's Kingship?", in *Concilium*, vol. XI, *Who is Jesus of Nazareth?*, Glen Rock, N. J., 1965, p. 60; Shiner, *op. cit.*, p. 19; and Ong, *op. cit.*, p. 163.

[25] Quoted in Mooney, *op. cit.*, p. 197.

ously. Part of the reason for this was undoubtedly the Thomistic position on the motive of the Incarnation. If Adam had not sinned, the word would not have become flesh. If this were the case, it is difficult to give more than a *qualified* primacy to the role of Christ in the whole of creation.[26]

One of the areas from which contemporary pressure is being exerted for producing a deeper theology here is the biblical renewal, especially in taking Saint Paul at his word. But, by coincidence, the very same task is being called for as a result of modern science. In a way, the lack of past development might be considered a boon, since now the task is not so much the alteration of a traditional Christology as the creation of a truly cosmic approach.

Dissatisfaction with particular elements of Teilhard de Chardin's effort in this regard should not be allowed to obscure how accurately he realized what was called for and how ingeniously he attempted to meet the need. Even the telling criticism of Hans Urs von Balthasar, that he does not seem to give any proper place to death or the cross, loses much of its force if one takes into account Karl Rahner's theology of death, for instance, in which the hypothesis is presented that the whole universe may take the place of the individual body in its relation to the soul at the time of death. In that case, Christ's death would be the occasion for His humanity's becoming fully active in the very depths of the cosmos as a redemptive power superior to all else.[27] Such notions, hypothetical and foreign as they are in our stunted Christology, must nonetheless receive at least an honest and sympathetic hearing. As Walter Ong reminds us:

> Theology has been severely handicapped in its exploration of the Incarnation of the Son because it has had to set this Incarnation against the backdrop of a universe very inadequately and even falsely conceived. . . . A Christology of an evolving cosmos lies ahead today as one of the greatest challenges which Christian theological speculation has ever had to meet.[28]

This, then, is the major challenge for today's theologian who would attempt to do justice to the impact of the Incarnation on our *Umwelt*. But at the same time, we are very much aware of

[26] See Riedlinger, *op. cit.*, p. 61.
[27] *Ibid.*
[28] Ong, *op. cit.*, pp. 163 ff.

mounting pressure for taking the consequences of the Incarnation more seriously in the realm of our *Mitwelt*, our relations with others. Our dissatisfaction with and rejection of certain recent attempts to reformulate the Christian faith that seem in the end to injure it more should not blind us to what is valid in their inspiration. Honest concern for the world, especially for the *Mitwelt*, the world of people, is central, and at least some of today's radical theology is a type of protest against Christian failure to take the gospel seriously. This is obvious in William Hamilton when he calls for a "radical" Christology which involves both an "unmasking" of Jesus Who is hidden in the world and a "becoming" Jesus in and to the world.[29] So, too, Thomas Altizer can say that the confession of Christ

> . . . directs us to the center of the world, into the heart of the profane, with the announcement that Christ is present here and he is present nowhere else. Once we confess that Christ is fully present in the moment before us, then we can truly love the world and can embrace even its pain and darkness as an epiphany of the body of Christ.[30]

We may take exception to ever so many things that these men are saying, and find unacceptable the ease with which they jettison the work of our forefathers in the faith. But for all that, they will have served a highly commendable purpose if they succeed in embarrassing us out of our *ecclesiocentrism*[31] into a fully incarnational approach to humanity, not in the abstract but in the concrete, as in the judgment scene in *Matthew*, "I was hungry and you gave *me* to eat."

It seems to me that what is required for a real breakthrough is

[29] See the treatment in Thomas W. Ogletree, *The Death of God Controversy*, Nashville, Abington Press, 1966, p. 38.

[30] Thomas J. J. Altizer, *The Gospel of Christian Atheism*, Philadelphia, Westminister Press, 1966, pp. 155 ff. See also Ogletree, *op. cit.*, p. 98.

[31] On the problem of ecclesiocentrism, see the stimulating article by John J. Harmon, "Toward a Theology of the City Church," *Cross Currents*, Fall, 1964, pp. 401-415; the observations of Yves Congar, O.P., in the collection of texts commenting on the *Constitution on the Church*, *Meditations on the Church*, New York, Herder and Herder, 1967, pp. 35 ff., regarding the transcendent character of the gospel and the Christian faith; and the ideas of William Stringfellow, *A Private and Public Faith*, Grand Rapids, Wm. B. Eerdmans Publishing Co., 1962: ". . . the churches are in reality almost wholly committed to serving their own existence" (p. 29).

not an outright rejection of the past but an intelligent appreciation of its shortcomings and of the consequent adjustment that must be made. In brief, we need a truly *"secular" ecclesiology*, one that assures the world-directed character of the Church, its all-consuming love of and concern for humanity, rather than one that concentrates on the Church itself, its structures, and its own preservation. As long as we think in terms like "perfect society," obviously we conceive the Church primarily in the same categories as the state or any other institution or organization. The solution is not to deny the organizational or institutional in the Church totally, but to shade it back to the secondary place it should hold.

The grounds for this adjustment are certainly present in the documents of Vatican II. To think first of the Church as a *sign* certainly eliminates any possible opposition to the *Mitwelt.* The very first section of Vatican II's greatest achievement, the *Constitution on the Church*, calls the Church "a kind of sacrament or sign of intimate union with God, and of the *unity of the whole human race.* She is also an instrument for the achievement of such union and unity." Two further splendid statements which can serve for the whole necessary reorientation are in the *Constitution on the Church in the Modern World.* The first, in section 76, says, "[The Church] is at once a sign and a safeguard of the transcendence of the *human person.*" If this concept was applied in practice, it would revolutionize many a chancery, parish, university, and other similar Church-related enterprise. The second, in section 92, says, ". . . the Church stands forth as a sign of that *brotherliness* which allows honest dialogue and invigorates it."

A sign is a sign as long as it points beyond itself to something more important, that which it exists to signify and, in the case of a sacrament, to bring about. And the Church of Vatican II, by her own admission, claims to be a sign standing for (1) the unity of mankind, (2) the transcendent value of the human person, and (3) the brotherliness on which dialogue thrives. The implications of these startling statements are so far-reaching that they call for at least an attitudinal revolution. The Church as a sign points beyond itself, witnessing to the fact that in God's intention it is meant to be co-terminous with the world, the *Mitwelt*, the family of man. This is to take quite seriously and much more literally than at times in the past the Pauline doctrine of Christ, the second Adam, Christ, the New Creation. Jesus is the really true man, the first utterly human ideal, man as God intends him to be. By sharing His life through the Spirit, we are not taken out of the world of men but more deeply involved in what it really means to be human.

The Church thus is not a separate family, not a ghetto, not a sect that draws us aside from the human family. It is the sign of God's plan for mankind, the sacrament of human unity, demonstrating by anticipation what God holds in store for all men, but admittedly doing so now only partially, imperfectly, in a way that requires ever further fulfillment. In this perspective, it becomes obvious that the Church exists *for* the world, for humanity. "*Sacramenta propter homines.*" The Father does not have a plan for the Church; He is not interested in Christians as such. His interest is in mankind, His plan is for mankind, and the Church is the sign, the sacramental expression of His concern for men.

It is important to stress that this is drawn from revelation, not from sociology or some *Zeitgeist.* Christ is God's Word expressed in human form, and His cross is the instrument for breaking down all the barriers of sin that separate men from God and from one another. The Church is the visible realm of His continuing work of reconciliation and peace for those who are far off and those who are near. Therefore, if we want to know what the Church's attitude and interests should be ideally, we need only look to the first chapters of *Genesis* to see what God's attitude and interests are. And throughout those early chapters, God's crowning interest is in *man,* with whom He desires to share His life. Could the Church's interest be other?

Any movement within the Church that retreats from humanity in favor of a closed group is a violation of the Church's sacramental nature and a denial of its catholicity. For example, an insidious nationalism can make it appear to the world that the Church is more interested in supporting and blessing any country's military onslaught than in witnessing mightily to the primacy of peace in her scale of values. A stance like this totally obscures the Church's nature as a sign of human brotherhood, and so widens the credibility gap that the world is fully justified in concluding that whether or not God is dead, such a Church certainly is.

My suggestion from all this is that perhaps the sign character of the Church is the key to a more integrated view of the relation between the incarnational and eschatological. The polarity, to be sure, neither has been nor should be resolved; but it should be brought out that there is an intimate relationship, a central continuity between the *even now* and the *not yet. Even now* the Church is the sign commissioned to anticipate, demonstrate, and strive mightily to achieve in all her activities that unity and brotherhood, that personalism and dialogue which have *not yet* reached fullness. In this perspective, the only time the incarnational is put in opposition to the eschatological is when the sign becomes a lie: when it no longer points effectively to the end that is its whole *raison d'être*, when it becomes a billboard on life's congested highway calling attention to all sorts of interim commodities, from fertility calendars to bingo prizes, but in its whole style of life gives no living witness to the real redemptive, unifying love of Christ.

In closing, I would like simply to allude to another entire area that becomes our central concern in this perspective. With the stress on the Church as sign in one of the four final documents of Vatican II, the *Constitution on the Church in the Modern World*, the cycle back to the first document, the *Constitution on the Sacred Liturgy*, is complete. This sign of human unity and fraternity that is the Church finds fullest expression and realization in the assembling to break the bread that proclaims the death of the Lord until He comes. The liturgy in our renewed theology emerges as having an importance that can be paralleled only by the measure of our neglect of it in the past.

Everything we have seen and said about the need for a so-called secular Christology, and more recently a secular ecclesiology, descends with a resounding thud at this point to force us to recognize the crying need for a "*secular liturgy*"—that is, a way of celebrating the presence and action of Christ *in* and *for* the world for which He died and rose again. Serious Christians in a world "come of age" will not much longer tolerate our "playing church." In a way, we can largely agree with men like Father Gommar de Pauw that the present situation tends to border on the ludicrous; for the only thing worse than no reform of the liturgy is half-reform.

It is true, let me quickly add, that a transition of such mammoth proportions requires time. But it should also be noted that time is at a premium. In a generation characterized by the revolution of rising expectations, we cannot have a council draw back the veil on the lost riches of our heritage and present an enthralling description of them to us in sixteen official documents, and then concoct only selected tidbits to nibble on.

The basic issue, then, immediately becomes the question of honesty. Are we serious, or are we playing games? If the Church is what it says it is, if its relation and mission to the world is truly this sacramental one, if the liturgy is its realization *par excellence*, then we have not only the right but the solemn duty to do all in our power to remove from the liturgy every barnacle of formalism, every façade that conceals its sign nature, every barrier that lessens its being a true experience of brotherhood in Jesus Christ, every artificial element that depersonalizes and dehumanizes its celebration, every gesture or garment that in any way contributes to the creation of an atmosphere of unreality or inauthenticity. If this is secularization, so be it, but it happens to be the prime necessity if the Church is to be truly the Church in the modern world. Because the liturgy is the fullest possible experience of the *not yet–even now*, it is here that eschatology and Incarnation become one in joyful celebration.

SISTER M. REMBERT HUBING, O.S.F.

17 Theology and the Arts

The spirit of an age addresses the world through its art and its worship. The early Church found the art of its times so expressive of pagan culture that it felt a strong impulse to reject art. In fact, it did so for some four hundred years. I often wonder how the Christian world would have treated Saint Jerome and his translation of the Bible if the Church had not recognized the need to keep the Christian imagination alive.

Nietzsche has a good statement about the revelatory power of artists as those who unveil secrets. He says:

> Only artists hate this slovenly life in borrowed manners and loosely fitting opinions and unveil the secret, everybody's bad conscience, the principle that every human being is a unique wonder; they dare to show us the human being as he is, down to the last muscle, himself and himself alone—even more, that in this rigorous consistency of his uniqueness he is beautiful and worth contemplating, as novel and incredible as every work of nature, and by no means dull.[1]

Art is an expression of the culture of a people. The artist voices the ethos of a society. He is a mediator of its inmost spirit, the celebrant of its values. If we would know Athens, we not only study its battles and politics but gaze at its Parthenon. To investigate the Middle Ages is to look at its Gothic cathedrals. To see America as it is today, we need to search through the selling galleries of New York, the international center of art since 1940.

[1] Quoted in Roger L. Shinn, "The Artist as Prophet-Priest of Culture," in Finley Eversole, ed., *Christian Faith and the Contemporary Arts*, Nashville, Abingdon Press, 1962, p. 167.

Alan Solomon, visiting professor of art at Cornell University and the organizer of the first New York "happening," has this to say about the art of the last twenty years in America:

> From time to time, those who take comfort in the presence of humans in art have found momentary hope in the emergence of new images of man. However, contemporary man sees himself in his art not as an idealized godlike figure in the manner of the classical tradition, but as a disrupted, contorted victim of the modern cataclysm, torn by forces of a magnitude beyond his comprehension, a grim figure, full of despair and anguish, entirely without hope.[2]

The appeal of today's artist is directly to the senses, visceral rather than intellectual.

Formerly, objects used in art had a "moral value." Food and culinary art comprised a still life; now plumbing tools are used. Books and musical instruments formed the older compositions, but these are replaced by comic strips and radio parts. The oversized hamburger and hot dog replace fruits and vegetables. Yet hot dogs, candy bars, Campbell's soup cans, pies, or Seven-Up bottles are not used as emotive devices.

The Cubists selected familiar, intimate, comfortable objects. The new artists select things familiar, public, and disquieting. In it all there is little of satire, social criticism, or snobbery, but an unqualified affirmation or commitment to the present environment with a consciousness of the triumph of feeling as the evaluative criterion over the material rational world. Contemporary artists are "feelers," not intellectuals.

All of this has followed a natural course which makes it an absolute product of our time. Today's artists live in a world financially smoother because they enjoy a larger sympathetic audience. They have withdrawn from institutional associations. They are not interested in philosophies as such. They share an innate passion for direct experience and reject all previous aesthetic canons.

Existentialism challenged many of the most cherished values, assumptions, theories, and beliefs of the nineteenth and twentieth centuries. But contemporary artists have not challenged standards. They have rejected them. Standards seem wholly lost. The critics'

[2] Alan Solomon, "The New Art," in Gregory Battcock, ed., *The New Art: A Critical Anthology,* New York, E. P. Dutton & Co., 1966, p. 68.

fear of failing to recognize originality has led them to accept shoddy absurdities. They dare reject nothing.

Leo Steinberg, an associate professor of art at Hunter College and lecturer at the Museum of Modern Art in New York, comments on contemporary art:

> The rapid domestication of the outrageous is the most characteristic feature of our artistic life, and the time lag between shock received and thanks returned gets progressively shorter. . . . Contemporary art is constantly inviting us to applaud the destruction of values which we still cherish, while the positive cause, for the sake of which the sacrifices are made, is rarely made clear, so that the sacrifices appear as acts of demolition, or of dismantling without any motive.[3]

It is misleading to say that the styles of art today do not last very long, because collectively they have been with us for a half-century. The thrill of pain once felt soon becomes an addiction. This is so true that societies like Soviet Russia's, whose art lacks this triumph of feeling over reason, seem only half-alive, unable to connect with the vital current of contemporary imagination. Thomas B. Hess, editor of *Art News*, says that contemporary painting has only one significance: it is new.

Yesterday's art enjoyed as patrons the kings and rulers of nations and the princes of the Church. The artist knew what was expected and worked with this content in mind. Today's patrons of the arts are a heterogeneous mass public and a closely knit ruling upper-middle class which has never been interested in art. This vanguard audience has been sympathetically involved with the artists, but for its own ends. It retains allegiance to and roots in the political status quo. The art world is its amusement place, its colorful social milieu. At cocktail parties, it looks for the person-artist and his foibles rather than his art. The vanguard audience needs acquisitions for its social status. It is a novelty pressure group whose taste is unformed and unsettled; the sales record is the passport to the validation of art.

De Stael, a contemporary painter who recently took his own life, often complained that a great cause of his anguish was that his pictures kept selling faster and at higher prices while he felt more

[3] Leo Steinberg, "Contemporary Art and the Plight of Its Public," in Battcock, *op. cit.*, p. 31.

and more doubtful about their existence and about what he intended to do and produce.

It is hard to know whether we are civilized, but we are cultivated. From 1953 to 1960, spending on the arts rose 130 percent. In 1960, Americans spent more than twice as much on the arts as on recreation, and six times as much as on sports. The $3 billion culture market of 1964 is expected to double by 1967. The "in" status symbol is conspicuous aesthetics.

The Lytton Financial Corporation, with its California offices displaying $400,000 worth of art purchases, has this saying: "A thing of beauty is a profit forever." With enough wealth, we may be able to have a cultural center on every corner, but we will not have the security of a forward-looking civilization. There is an ancient Oriental saying that when everyone recognizes beauty as beautiful, there is already ugliness.

A great art demands a great audience. The capacity for self-criticism is a criterion of human authenticity. Without it, smugness and self-satisfaction will blind man to himself.

Art can reveal the deepest roots of our existence, and through this revelation, man gives real sacramental form to his concepts of existence. The most meaningful act man can perform is to make the meaning of life visible.

Contemporary artists in their anguished contortions are striving to express some meaning. That they seem to be saying man is nothing is an indictment against Christianity today. Still, for all its pessimism and near-despair, their negation is not absolute. As Camus once said, "Even the work that negates still affirms something and does homage to the wretched and magnificent life that is ours."

The artist looks upon our world and dares to bring into consciousness the fear which lies in the soul of twentieth-century man: that life is meaningless.

Paul Tillich has often been quoted for his saying that Picasso's *Guernica* is the best present-day religious picture. The contorted fury of the picture is not only an expostulation against the cruel bombing of civilians in Spain; it exposes a human situation, the evil of injustices in war.

It is the wonder and mystery of art, as likewise of religion, that it reveals hidden reality. The biblical concept of truth is mystery to be uncovered or discovered. While the arts uncover for us the character of particular things in the starkness of their being, they discover truth.

It is the responsibility of the artist to present the concrete with great intensity, isolated and enhanced, so that it will be accessible and comprehensible to others in a way seldom otherwise possible to them. Further, the concrete reality is presented so that its significance is seen as flowing from its relation to other things. Hegel calls this the "concrete universal." Creative imagination is precisely the power to reveal the universal in the particular.

The theology of the past, with its emphasis on the divinity of Christ to the neglect of His humanity, has done a disservice to mankind. As Christ became more and more isolated from man through the overemphasis on His divinity, man failed to recognize the glory of his own humanity as revelatory of the Father.

The Gothic cathedrals, a product of this thirteenth-century thought, made man a very small, insignificant creature in a massively high house of worship. In reaction, the Renaissance man evidenced a false sense of his humanity in seeking out the culture of Greece and Rome because his theologians denied him the fullness of the humanity of Christ, which is his humanity.

Today's stress on the fullness of the human knowledge and faith of Christ presents man in the image of His own glory in being fully human.

Theologians must involve themselves in gaining a fresh insight into the human condition that the artist is grappling with. If they do not pay heed to the wrestling of the creative artist, they may well find that Christian thought is incapable of meeting the deeper significance of the times. The Church has a great need for her theology to make a charismatic search into the aspirations of the people of the times as revealed in the stark reports, prophecies, and events that the arts of our times are emitting. The Christian community would do well to become aware of the needs of the artists in their search for meanings and in their struggles, and not abandon them because they do not believe that society will ever become worthwhile. Let us avoid the mistake the early Church made in rejecting the arts because it found them too pagan.

The contemporary artist desperately needs the understanding and help of the contemporary theologian. It may well be that the vital step in this "crisis of faith" must be taken by the theologian: to look to the artist as a source of the revelation of God at this moment and for his contemporary awareness of man. The breach between art and theology today is so great that only a bridge built by the theologian can restore communication. The theologian must invite the artist.

But let the theologian not think that the service will be all on his side, for as Nathan Scott says:

> . . . the creativity of the artist is calculated very greatly to enhance the creativity of religion, for in the creative forces of authentic art the religious community will find an indispensable ally in promoting the health of the imagination, apart from which the integrity of man can in no wise be guaranteed. And, since the order of sensibility does not lie immediately within the special purview of the theologian, he cannot but regard the artist as one of his most natural partners.[4]

[4] Nathan A. Scott, Jr., *The Broken Center*, New Haven, Yale University Press, 1965, p. 192.

REV. GERARD A. VANDERHAAR, O.P.

18 Theological Implications of Theories About the Universe

Theology is concerned with God's revelation to man in the context of salvation. Since God reveals himself to man and saves him in man's existential situation, theology must be concerned with that situation, with the world in which man lives and meets God and is saved.

When God first revealed himself, it was easy to picture him as our Father in heaven, looking down with love on his children, who occupied a privileged place in a small world. The scene was compact. The world was a flat surface, topped by the dome of the firmament in which moved "the greater light to rule the day and the smaller one to rule the night and . . . the stars" (Gen. 1:16). Today, however, the setting of revelation and salvation is a vast universe, stretching out from the earth in every direction almost limitlessly. We know that there are some 100,000 million billion stars in the universe, of which our sun is only one. This means that God is not just our Father in heaven by Creator and Lord of an expanse which is so large that we cannot even imagine it. And man is only a tiny speck of precarious life on a satellite of one of those 100,000 million billion stars, and realizes that his privileged position at the center of creation is a primitive myth.

Still, the basic elements of theology remain: God chose to reveal himself to man and to invite us to fellowship with himself.[1] Only now we see that it is all happening in a completely different cosmological context from what we pictured when we first became aware

[1] *Dogmatic Constitution on Divine Revelation,* sec. 2.

of it. I would like to take up three theological problems raised by contemporary scientific theories about the size and constitution of the universe: first, the doctrine of creation and how it fits in with current scientific speculation about the origin of this immense and dynamic universe; second, the question of the possibility of life elsewhere in the universe; and third, the need for God in the light of scientific cosmology.

Creation

There are two principal scientific notions about the origin of the universe: the so-called "big bang" theory and the "steady state" theory. The big bang theory was developed after a significant discovery made in 1925 by Edwin Hubble at the Mount Wilson Observatory in California. Hubble found that some stars originally presumed to be in our own galaxy of the Milky Way were in reality part of another galaxy as large as our own and extremely far away from us. By applying to this discovery the phenomenon of the red shift, Hubble determined that these distant galaxies were speeding away from us and from each other. The red shift, which is the movement of the characteristic lines on the color spectrum toward the red or longer wave lengths, is a peculiarity of light similar to the familiar phenomenon of the sound of a train whistle dropping in pitch (because its wave length is increased) as the train speeds away from the listener at the railroad station. The scientific interpretation was that "The entire space of the universe, populated by billions of galaxies, is in a state of rapid expansion, with all its members flying away from one another at high speed." [2]

If the universe is now expanding, it must follow that in the past the galaxies were closer together. In a mental reversal of the process of expansion, it was supposed that about 10 billion years ago, all the matter in the universe was crowded into a relatively small area, a huge primordial atom of electrons, protons, and neutrons. At that time, the evolutionary process began, resembling a nuclear explosion at first. Over a period of billions of years, the process resulted in the stars and planets we know and in at least one planet which is the home of the highly complex intelligent life of which we are a part.

[2] George Gamow, *The Creation of the Universe*, rev. ed., New York, Viking Press, 1961, p. 23.

There is a variation on the big bang theory: the theory of the oscillating universe. It would have the initial explosion caused by a rushing together of all the matter of the universe from far-distant points. After the explosion, the expansion continues until the momentum is lost, and the contraction begins again. Each cycle, it is estimated, would take about eighty billion years.[3]

An alternative to the big bang hypothesis is the steady state theory, developed by, among others, the British astronomer Fred Hoyle. According to this explanation, the universe has always looked the same as it does now, even though it has always been expanding as it is now. To fill in the gaps caused by the expansion, new matter is continuously being created throughout space. The universe is eternal, and the rate of creation of new matter need not be very high to compensate for the expansion: only one hydrogen atom per liter of space every billion years.[4]

Of these theories, the steady state seems to be on the weakest scientific grounds right now. Astronomers tend toward accepting some variation of the argument that the universe as we know it began from an initial event which started everything off.

The theological question concerns the relationship of these theories with the revealed doctrine of God's creation of the world. It is not necessary here to review the biblical and magisterial teachings on creation.[5] The primary point of the dogma of creation is that the world, the universe, is dependent on God for its being. To be created is to be dependent, to exist because of another, because of God. As Karl Rahner and Herbert Vorgrimler put it, the createdness of the world is "its permanent rootedness in the free enactment of the personal God, whereby the world, totally and at all times, remains dependent on him." [6]

Although continual dependence on God is the primary truth in the doctrine of creation, the Church has taught that there was an actual beginning, that God created *ab initio temporis*, from the beginning of time.[7] This does not mean that at a certain point in

[3] *Time*, "Science," March 11, 1966, p. 82.

[4] Gamow, *op. cit.*, p. 32.

[5] See Trophime Mouiren, "The Creation," in *Twentieth-Century Encyclopedia of Catholicism*, New York, Hawthorn Books, 1962, Vol. XIX, Chap. 2.

[6] Karl Rahner and Herbert Vorgrimler, *Theological Dictionary*, New York, Herder and Herder, 1965, p. 106.

[7] ". . . God by His goodness and omnipotent power . . . immediately

time God performed his creative act, as if there was already a time before the world began, but rather that time itself began with creation. What is clearly implied here is the non-eternity of the universe.[8]

When the scientific theories are correctly understood, they do not seem to conflict with the doctrine of creation. Science can say nothing about dependence on God, the primary truth of creation. Neither can science determine whether the universe is eternal; eternity by definition can never be measured. In not finding a satisfactory beginning, which theories other than that of the primitive explosion do not, science does not contradict the doctrine of creation, because we have no guarantee from faith that the *initium temporis* will ever be scientifically discoverable.

In the same vein, it would be rash for theologians to smile triumphantly because the big bang theory now seems to dominate the scientific scene, as though science is finally coming around to our side. The initial explosion which this theory postulates may not be the absolute beginning, and, unlikely as it seems now, there may have been a great deal of created existence before it, as the theory of the oscillating universe proposes.

Life Elsewhere in the Universe

The second problem concerns the possibility that intelligent life exists somewhere in the universe besides earth, long a favorite science fiction theme. Many scientists say this is a significant possibility, and some go so far as to postulate highly advanced technical societies in the universe.[9] This line of thought is based fundamentally on two assumptions: (1) the origin of life can be explained by natural processes, most of which are already known and which will inevitably occur whenever the chemistry, geology, and climate are right; and (2) the universe contains such a tremendous number of

---

from the beginning of time fashioned each creature out of nothing, spiritual and corporeal, namely angelic and mundane" (Vatican I, *Dogmatic Constitution Concerning the Catholic Faith*, Denzinger 1783, Chap. 1).

[8] See Thomas Aquinas, *Summa Theologiae*, I, q. 46, a. 1; Louis Bouyer, *Dictionary of Theology*, New York, Desclee, 1965, p. 105; and Mouiren, *op. cit.*, p. 112.

[9] See I. S. Shklovskii and Carl Sagan, *Intelligent Life in the Universe*, San Francisco, Holden-Day, 1966, p. 379.

stars that it is probable that many planets have the exact same life-giving conditions as earth.

The second point is based on statistical analysis. There are nine known planets in our solar system. Our sun is a member of an enormous collection of stars in the Milky Way, which is our galaxy. It is estimated that the Milky Way comprises over 100 billion (10^{11}) stars of various types and ages, many of which could have a planetary system like ours.[10] But the Milky Way is only one galaxy in the universe. Scientists think that there are actually billions of galaxies like this one,[11] making the total number of stars in the universe more than 100,000 million billion (10^{20}). Assuming rigid conditions of suitability, so that perhaps only one star out of a million million meets all the requirements for having a planet which can sustain life, the number of stars is so astronomically high that this still leaves 100 million (10^{8}) planetary systems suitable for organic life. Statistically, many planets among the systems would have the conditions necessary for the development of intelligent life.

Other scientists, however, are not impressed by statistical procedures like these. Observing the workings of evolution here on earth, they point out that man's existence depends on a very precise sequence of causative events through some 2 billion years, and that part of the causal chain was random or accidental events. Hence, repetition of the sequence is virtually impossible, even granted the large number of stars in existence.[12]

Theologically, the greatest problem raised by the possible existence of intelligent life elsewhere in the universe is the Incarnation. Is Jesus of Nazareth the unique Incarnation of God in the cosmos, or could other intelligent creatures be so favored? On the uncertain supposition that such life exists (of which there is not one shred of real evidence), it is quite possible that God revealed himself in a way which might have included Incarnation. Rahner and Vorgrimler say that in the Incarnation, "God assumes a reality which is other than his own and makes it the manifestation of his own truly

[10] See Harlow Shapley, *Of Stars and Men*, New York, Washington Square Press, 1959, p. 66; and Shklovskii and Sagan, *op. cit.*, p. 29.

[11] See Hannes Alfven, *Worlds—Antiworlds*, San Francisco, W. H. Freeman & Co., 1966, p. 9; Gamow, *op. cit.*, p. 23; and Shapley, *op. cit.*, p. 64.

[12] G. G. Simpson, *This View of Life*, New York, Harcourt, Brace & World, 1964, p. 267.

self-declaratory presence."[13] God could choose to reveal himself to any other race of intelligent beings, just as he has done for us. If he did so, if there was another Incarnation, this would mean that Jesus Christ is not the center, the climax of creation, although he will still be the alpha and omega of *human* existence.

The Need for God

A third theological question concerns the need to have recourse to God in order to explain the origin and constitution of things. The mysteries of creation, of life, of human life are all becoming increasingly illuminated by contemporary scientific advances, and there are those who echo the reply Laplace is said to have made when Napoleon questioned him about God's place in his theory of the planets' origin: "I have no need of that hypothesis." Scientific progress is being made today without reference to God to explain the origin and condition of the universe.[14] Bonhoeffer has spoken of this: "Man has learned to cope with all questions of importance without recourse to God as a working hypothesis."[15] God is pushed farther and farther back by the expanding boundaries of human knowledge. A world come of age thinks it can get along without him.

Michael Novak has suggested that a key to the theology of secularity is the traditional Scholastic distinction between primary and secondary causality.[16] According to this distinction, God as the primary cause is present to all things, intimately involved in their being and operation, which cannot take place without him. But the secondary causes to which he is present have their own integrity, their own reality, which from one point of view is the sole source of the effects which take place. God as primary cause is no *deus ex machina*, stepping in from time to time to cause things which otherwise would not happen. As primary cause of all things, he influences them to act in their own natural ways, so that if only the natural is investigated, God is completely hidden.

[13] Rahner and Vorgrimler, *op. cit.*, p. 78.
[14] See, for example, Shapley, *op. cit.*, pp. 4, 5, 14, 22; and Alfven, *op. cit.*, p. 3.
[15] Dietrich Bonhoeffer, *Letters and Papers from Prison*, New York, Macmillan Company, 1962, paperback, p. 195.
[16] In *National Catholic Reporter*, September 29, 1965, p. 6.

It may very well be that the scientist will never need the hypothesis of God to explain the universe, because the scientist is totally concerned with what we would call secondary causes and because he is not, as scientist, looking at the dependence we call creation. The Swedish physicist Hannes Alfven, writing about how the universe arose, what its purpose is, and what exists beyond it, says that perhaps we shall never know the answers for certain, and that these questions may be "essentially meaningless" to a scientist.[17]

Such attitudes clash with the desire many people have today to believe in a God. The pace of world events is too great, the threats of disaster too ominous for the ordinary person. There is a strong tendency for us to believe in an omnipotent, omniscient, and loving God, a God who is concerned with our predicament, who gives some assurance of our survival, but who is explicable within the framework of contemporary science. Some of the stories associated with flying saucers—kindly beings from another planet, concerned about the inhabitants of earth, and able to use their technological skills to save us from ourselves—seem to be expressions of this tendency. The saucer myths, it has been suggested, represent a neat compromise between the need to believe in a traditional, paternal God and the contemporary pressures to accept the pronouncements of science.[18]

Conclusion

Scientific theories about the universe in the past hundred years seem to be a curious mixture of certainty and speculation. On the one hand, there has been an impressive increase in our knowledge of how big it is and how it is likely to have started. On the other, the evidence supporting these theories is scanty. Scientists assume that the same natural laws are at work in the universe which have been discovered on earth: laws of gravity, of electricity, of chemical composition, of relativity. The available evidence gives weight to this assumption, but because the substantiations are admittedly meager, the grand extrapolation seems at times to be tenuous.[19] And

[17] Alfven, *op. cit.*, p. 3.
[18] Shklovskii and Sagan, *op. cit.*, p. 19.
[19] Raymond J. Nogar, O.P., "The Mystery of Cosmic Epigenesis," *American Catholic Philosophical Association Proceedings,* 1965, p. 115.

yet, until there is evidence to the contrary, the new theories must control the day.

Theology, too, is a mixture of certainty and speculation: certainty of the God who has revealed himself unto salvation, and speculation about much of the human consequences of that revelation. At times in the past, theology has been more certain than the situation warranted, often with unfortunate effects. Scientists are justifiably wary of the dogmatic religionist, the theological imperialist. But scientists generally are aware of their own limitations, and know that the ultimate consequences of their theories can rightfully be explored only by philosophers and theologians. Shapley writes, ". . . the task of the proper scientist is to bring forth and explain as best he can the raw materials from which other analyzers can fabricate philosophies."[20] Alfven's "essentially meaningless" set of questions is "a matter for the philosopher to determine," he says, "for it falls outside the scientists purview."[21]

Here is today's challenge to theology. Science has had to break away painfully from the domination of theologians, and has pushed the frontiers of human knowledge back breathtaking distances. It is now up to the philosopher and theologian to make use of these findings and theories in elaborating valuable hypotheses which attempt to answer the ultimate questions. The days of theological interference are, we hope, over. As Cardinal Suenens said in another context, one Galileo case is enough for the Church.[22] The days of theological opportunity are here. We can say today somewhat more literally that the sky is the limit.

[20] Shapley, *op. cit.*, p. 126.
[21] Alfven, *op. cit.*, p. 3.
[22] Speech at the fourth session of Vatican II, quoted in *National Catholic Reporter,* November 11, 1964, p. 6.

VII Conclusion

This, therefore, I say and testify in the Lord, that henceforward you are not to walk as the Gentiles walk in the futility of their mind, having their understanding clouded in darkness, estranged from the life of God through the ignorance that is in them, because of the blindness of their heart.

EPHESIANS 4:17-18

LESLIE DEWART

19 Autonomy: The Key Word in Secularism

It is hardly necessary to defend the importance of the topic of academic freedom and religious commitment. On the contrary, because it is so important, it seems to have been almost exhaustively discussed. Most Catholics have reached their conclusions about this issue; sometimes it seems as if the only real problem left were a predominantly practical one: how to deal effectively and (preferably) peacefully with those of the opposite persuasion.

Yet, this is evidently not a desirable situation. Even when these divisions do not produce conflict and political struggles—and it is scarcely informative to mention that much too often they do—the hardening of positions cannot be beneficial to the Church. These divisions mean, at best, lessened communication and diminished mutual sympathy and esteem. Surely we must attempt to reverse this trend. Perhaps the time has come to shift to a new level of discussion.

Let us, then, put the question to rest: whether the dissident believer ought to be institutionally and otherwise accorded (or denied) the freedom of thought which may (or may not) rightfully belong to him. Let us acknowledge the repetitiousness of debates on the nature and extent of the limits which must be imposed on the academic freedom of individuals for the sake of the common good of the Church. Let us instead ask ourselves: why do people who share the same faith and who, on the whole, must be supposed to be equally well-meaning, differ so drastically in their evaluation of the moral problems connected with the exercise of human thought? If communication is to increase, it might be more profitable for both traditionalists and progressives to determine why they differ, than for them to renew their attempt to justify to themselves, to each other, and to any bystanders who will listen whatever positions have been already occupied.

Now, it seems to me, generally speaking, both traditionalists and progressives have common objectives, which stem from common basic religious motives. Those who cluster around the restrictive pole of the field of opinion on this subject sometimes have little concern for the rights of others, or overestimate the relevance of legitimate authority. But this is by way of exception. Nor is it frequently the case that they who stand at the other end of the spectrum do so because they chafe at uncomfortable truths, or because they have succumbed to the Blandishments of Scandalous Falsehood Bedecked with the Deceptive Ornaments of Truth. Personal bewilderment candidly expressed, like the agony of decisions reluctantly taken, should manifest to traditionalist and progressive alike the conscientious, though possibly benighted, nature of each other's views. If we look honestly and carefully, we cannot escape the impression that all shades of opinion on this matter invariably depend upon a common concern for truth—predicated in turn upon a common act of faith in Christianity *as true*.

The root of the trouble, I suggest, can be traced to this common concern for the *truth* of faith. The specific difficulty is that some conceive the nature of knowledge, and therefore the nature of truth and of error, in a manner which requires them in good logic to fear for the safety of the truths of faith unless certain restrictive measures are taken, whereas others conceive truth and the intellect in a different way, from which it follows that academic or other intellectual restrictions are not merely unnecessary but even prejudicial to the cultivation of truth. For the latter, concern for the truth is not only compatible with the utmost academic freedom but actually demanding it. In short, whether permissive or restrictive, all views on academic freedom imply a certain concept of knowledge, truth, and error. Different moral conclusions stem from differences of the epistemic order.

I say *epistemic*, not *epistemological*, because these differences have to do not simply with the *theory* of knowledge but with the more fundamental *concept* of knowledge which epistemology elaborates.

In the Hellenic-western philosophical tradition, there have been many theories of knowledge dialectically succeeding one another as philosophers have developed and deepened their understanding of one concept of knowledge which remained fairly stable after the pre-Socratics. But this continuous development reached a critical point with Hegel, when a sort of qualitative change in the history of epistemology began to occur. After Hegel, a new conceptualization of the observable facts of knowledge gradually emerged—so gradually, indeed, that only with the hindsight of a century and a half can we begin to appreciate the quality of the change. Thus, within the continuity of our philosophical tradition from the Greeks to our own day, there are two principal concepts of knowledge: the classical and the contemporary. Whereas up to Hegel the variety of philosophies bespoke a continuity both in filiation and in common concept of what the fact of knowledge is, contemporary epistemologies exhibit only a continuity in filiation with those of the Greek, medieval, and early modern periods; they no longer share with the latter common assumptions about precisely what epistemology tries to understand and explain.

The observation from which all classical epistemologies started was an irreducible, entitative opposition between self and nonself, subject and object, mind and being as such. Knowledge was the overcoming of this opposition—somehow—in a union (of a surely nonphysical sort) effected by the knower in act. For Saint Thomas, for instance, knowledge occurred when one being acted transitively upon another which was endowed with the power to take advantage of this activity upon itself in order to posit within itself an immanent act whose formal nature was to render it (intentionally) one with the other (that is, an other which precisely as intentionally united to the knower remained other than it). Of course, the concept of intentionality introduced an interpretation into what we conceived knowledge to be, and even the philosophical definition of knowledge as "becoming the other as other" was the result of a long and arduous process of philosophical elaboration.

Nonetheless, this and other theories of knowledge commonly attempted to explain how two things which were distinct *in themselves*, two realities *independent of each other* in the order of being, happened to become *one for us*, one in the order of knowledge, or intentionally one. This becoming-one-for-us was what we called knowledge. The problems of psychology and epistemology had to do with the processes whereby and the conditions under which this type of event came to pass and became itself intelligible.

Now, the classical philosophers also observed that knowledge worked a certain perfection in us. There was an observable difference between him who did not know and him who knew. Knowledge had a certain *value;* for instance, it was worthy of being pursued and loved. This *valuable* aspect of knowledge was called *truth.* But if knowledge was the transcending of the subject-object opposition, truth must be conceived as some sort of relation of the mind to its object. Every question about the nature of this relation, the process whereby it accrued to the mind, or the conditions of its presence or absence remained the legitimate subject of further inquiry. Within this concept of truth, philosophers might intramurally discuss, for instance, whether truth was found in simple apprehension, judgment, or reasoning. Hence, questions of this sort might be controverted only within the assumption that, whatever else might be said of it, truth was some sort of conformity of the mind with what it knew. For surely no cognitive perfection followed, no value accrued to the mind in the act of knowing, if the act did not bring about the conformity of mind with being. Without this result, knowledge had failed; it had been attempted, but it had not come about. Though there had been, as it were, a promise of truth, the promise had not been fulfilled. The process of knowledge had aborted, and brought forth error instead of truth.

The history of philosophy has shown that there are difficulties with every variation of this type of epistemology. For present purposes, the most serious is a paradox: this understanding of truth cannot admit the true reality of error. It renders the failure of knowledge unintelligible in terms of the intellectual process itself. Conversely, it makes the intellect essentially infallible—and the difficulty with this, apart from its being very hard to reconcile with experience, is that it is self-contradictory. For this idea of error leads to the complete identification of truth and knowledge—and this means, in the end, a denial of the reality of truth, that is, of the distinct value of knowledge. Ironically, the reality of truth is wedded to the reality of error.

Thus, in erroneous knowledge, there could be no conformity

with being, hence no truth, and therefore no knowledge properly so called. These epistemologies did not really attempt to explain the *error of knowledge*. What they sought to explain was the abortion of knowledge: how did it happen that the act which of its very nature should have resulted in truth issued instead in error, that is, failed to become truly an act of knowledge?

But once the question was posed in these terms, the answer had to find the explanation of error in something *extrinsic* to knowledge itself. In this view, error was never a real quality of knowledge, but something foreign to knowledge which somehow prevented knowledge from being truly itself.

The doctrine of Saint Thomas illustrates this well. Saint Thomas never once supposed that truth might be conceived except as the mind's conformity with being. The question "What is truth?" meant to him simply this: does the correspondence of being with the knowing power refer to something in the knower or to something in being? [1] We need not consider here his reply, but only the assumptions which remained unquestioned: that being as such is related to knowledge, and that truth is the homologous relation of the being of knowledge to being as such. This is why he found the explanation of error (insofar as he may be said to have found one) to lie in causes wholly extrinsic to knowledge itself. For instance, falsity in sense knowledge is due to such causes as a derangement of the organ or a disturbance of the medium. And error can be in the intellect insofar as its judgment "on what is presented by sense" is conditioned by the falsity of something outside the intellect, namely, the falsity of sense knowledge. Thus, "Sense always produces a true judgment in the intellect with respect to its own conditions, but not always with respect to the condition of things." [2] But in itself, intrinsically, the intellect cannot be deceived: "The proper object of the intellect . . . is the quiddity of a thing. Hence, just as the sensing of proper sensibles is always true, so the intellect is always true in knowing what a thing is. . . . By accident, however, falsity can occur in this knowing of quiddities, if the intellect falsely joins and separates." [3]

[1] See Thomas Aquinas, *De Veritate,* I, 1.

[2] *Ibid.*, I, 11.

[3] *Ibid.*, I, 12. Likewise, in relation to opining and reasoning, there can be falsity in the intellect—but only in a restricted sense, for this "never occurs if a reduction to first principles is made correctly" (*ibid.*).

Saint Thomas did not proceed to ask directly why this "accident," the false composition or division of the act of judgment, sometimes occurred and sometimes did not. In other words, he did not ask how error was possible, given its monstrous character. Nevertheless, we can estimate where his doctrine led, from his treatment of the question whether man could be deceived before the fall. His reply was unqualifiedly negative. In the absence of sin, there could be in the human intellect only ignorance, not error, "the absence of some knowledge, but no false opinion." We can deduce this from "the integrity of the primitive state." For "As truth is the good of the intellect, so falsehood is its evil." Now, in itself the intellect is infallible: "As regards its proper object, the intellect is ever true; and hence it is never deceived of itself." But it may be led astray "by a lower faculty," given the inner disorder of man after the fall. Evidently, had this disorder not been introduced by sin, error would never be found in the human intellect.[4]

I do not recall any text of Saint Thomas in which he considers what role, if any, the will plays in the abortion of knowledge. But in the light of the foregoing, especially if we also remember that in the context of faith Saint Thomas did assert that the will can determine the judgment to an inevident object,[5] it may be suggested that he opened the way for Descartes' attribution of error to the imprudent precipitance of a judgment determined by man's free will. In fact, at least one distinguished contemporary Thomist has thought that according to Saint Thomas, "There is no false judgment without sin." [6] If this statement refers to *actual* sin, it is probably an exaggeration. It would be better to say that this is the most logical conclusion to draw from the doctrine of Saint Thomas, although he himself did not draw it. But in respect to *original* sin, the assertion seems wholly warranted.

Likewise, it would be wholly incorrect to suppose that Saint Thomas' doctrine of truth and error led him to the idea that "error has no rights." But it would be warranted to think that the concepts of truth as conformity and of error as a cognitive abortion are the

[4] Thomas Aquinas, *Summa Theologiae,* I, 94, 4.

[5] *Ibid.*, IIa-IIae, 2, 1, ad. 3.

[6] M. D. Roland-Gosselin, "La Théorie thomiste de l'erreur," *Mélanges Thomistes*, Paris, 1923, p. 266; quoted in Jacques Maritain, *Trois Réformateurs,* Paris, 1925, p. 295.

conditions of the possibility of intellectual intolerance. To the degree that later ages have drawn their attitudes from and based their moral practice upon philosophies of knowledge which did not, to be sure, begin with Saint Thomas but which he perfected and codified, they have in all consistency concluded that there is no room for error within the community of those who believe in the truth revealed by God. Error is, in some sense and measure, due to sin. To countenance it is to countenance sin.

The crudest forms of this doctrine are no longer widely held. We can safely say, I think, that the burning of heretics is a thing of the past. Religious wars, though clearly obsolete, have not been so definitively rejected; even today they remain a distinct if remote possibility (at least in relation to certain forms of atheism). The trend is toward increasingly milder interpretations and more humane applications of the principle that error has no rights. Intolerance in the twentieth century speaks softly, and shuns harshness and violence. It has become civilized, and upon occasion it is overlaid with good manners and *politesse*.

I do not speak ironically. It is very widely recognized in today's Church that although error still has no rights, the errant person does. Many traditionalists insist that equal stress must be placed upon the preservation of truth, the extirpation of error, and the prevention of scandal on the one hand and upon the respect due the dissident's claims in justice on the other—and some of them go so far as to include under this heading the dissenter's personal right to private dissent. Maritain, I believe, belongs in this category.[7]

I may also quote other Thomists who not very long ago dismissed the problem of academic freedom as a pseudo-problem. The matter need never arise, they thought, if a distinction is made "between the teacher as teacher and the teacher as autonomous" scholar. As a private person, the teacher "has . . . a personal responsibility to truth itself." This is his private affair to conduct well or ill—at the peril of his soul, to be sure. But the teacher *as such* "undertakes to act as the college's committed representative in the classroom." In that guise, which by this reckoning is his proper academic guise, the teacher must conform with the academy's will that its view of

[7] See, e.g., Jacques Maritain, *The Range of Reason*, New York, Charles Scribner's Sons, 1952, p. 168.

the truth prevail—just as the academy itself, presumably through its supreme authority, "is subject to the teaching and ruling authority of the Church, and thus has the duty to follow the guidance of the Church in all areas of education and teaching." Nothing in these provisions, moreover, need conflict in the slightest with a properly understood academic freedom. For no one is forced to be a Catholic college teacher—or, for that matter, a member of the Church. Anyone who may wish to dissent remains free to leave his academic institution and/or the Church.[8]

The point I would stress here is not that these views can be controverted on a variety of grounds, such as their infantile understanding of the nature of legitimate religious authority, their naive theology of the nature of revealed truth, and their juridical, asocial, and ahistorical idea of the nature of the Church. The point is rather that to reject intellectual intolerance in kind, and not merely in degree, it is necessary to deal with the question at the root. The idea that "error has no rights" must be tackled as a principle of the epistemological order. It is at this juncture that contemporary Catholic thought may profit from the post-Hegelian emergence of a concept of knowledge which encompasses but also transcends the classical understanding of it as an act of intentional intussusception.

As I have suggested, the classical concept was based upon an undeniable and seemingly primary observation of a fact, namely, the irreducible, entitative opposition between self and nonself. But from the work of otherwise disparate thinkers during the last hundred years—I have in mind such as Kierkegaard, Marx, Nietzsche, James, Bergson, Dewey, Husserl, Heidegger, Sartre, Marcel, Berdyaev, and Wittgenstein—it has come to light that although the foregoing observation was indeed truly undeniable and even in a sense absolutely primary, its true undeniability and primacy had not been sufficiently appreciated during the first age of our philosophical history, which ran from the Greeks to Hegel. Paradoxically, the deeper value of this observation had been jeopardized by the classical failure to take account of something that almost everyone had said all along without actually realizing its importance and mean-

[8] The preposterous nature of some of these views may suggest that I have manufactured a man of straw. The fact is I have quoted and abstracted from an actual document, written in 1962, subscribed to by several Catholic philosophers who have not so far as I know repudiated these views at any later time.

ing: this undeniable and primary opposition of object and subject is indeed assertable and warranted because it is a matter of plain *observation*, a simple question of *empirical fact*.

We have tended to forget that empirical facts are observed facts, that to ground philosophy upon the observation of an irreducible, undeniable entitative opposition between subject and object is to ground it upon a *known* fact. Therefore, the primacy of this observation tells us something not only about the nature of being but also about the nature of knowledge. The first principle of epistemology is not, as we have assumed in the past, a statement of the *a priori* conditions of knowledge; it does not describe the pre-cognitive conditions that must obtain *before* knowledge can obtain (and before it can be thereafter examined by the knower). To repeat: we must take seriously the proposition that the opposition between subject and object *is* an empirical fact. For this proposition means: whenever we observe this opposition, knowledge has *already* come into being.

The contemporary concept of knowledge takes nothing away from the empirical fact which is the starting point of the classical epistemologies. But contemporary epistomologies *add* to it a crucial refinement, namely, taking account of the empirical fact that the empirical fact of knowledge *is* an empirical fact. Hence, the opposition of object and subject is not a fact of nature—I mean, it is not a fact prior to knowledge. On the contrary, it is posterior to knowledge. Hence, knowledge is not the overcoming of an original dichotomy but, on the contrary, the introduction of a dichotomy into what was originally undifferentiated. Knowledge is that within which and in consequence of which the opposition of object and subject can appear. Knowledge is the condition of the possibility of the opposition of subject and object. Berdyaev has compressed this idea into a lucid paragraph:

> The dogmatic ontology of the Greek and the medieval philosophy could not resist the critique of reason, and it is impossible to return to the pre-critical forms of philosophizing. Even modern Thomism, which refuses to recognize Descartes and indeed the whole of modern philosophy, is nevertheless bound to be neo-Thomism and to pass through critical reflection. The point is that the critique of knowledge, the reflection of reason upon itself, is not the abstract theory which it claims to be, but a living experience. However strongly knowledge may contrast itself with

> life and doubt the possibility of knowing life, it is itself a part of life; it is generated by life and reflects its destinies. The same thing is true of epistemological thought. . . . The opposition between knowledge and existence, regarded as an object standing over against the knowing subject, is not primary but secondary, and is the result of reflection. The primary fact is that knowledge itself is a reality and takes place in reality. . . . If we rise to a spiritual conception of knowledge, we shall see that knowledge is an act in and through which something happens to reality. Reality is illumined through knowledge. It is not a case of someone or something cognizing being as a separate and independent object: being cognizes itself, and through this cognition expands and is lit up from within. . . . A cleavage takes place in reality, and in knowledge it expresses itself as objectivization.[9]

As the concept of knowledge has developed, the concepts of truth and error have undergone a corresponding elaboration. To assert the inadequacy of the concept of truth as the conformity of the mind with being is not to suggest that the converse is true, namely, that truth is the conformity of things in themselves with the mind (as unsophisticated critics of contemporary thought sometimes suppose). For it would be absurd to suppose that true knowledge could obtain by the mind's arbitrary affirmation of "what is" regardless of what things might be "in themselves"; this very supposition requires that things be "in themselves" whatever they are, independently of what we may arbitrarily affirm. No philosopher, to my knowledge, has ever sugested this. There can be little doubt that when knowledge is true, the logical relation of the mind to being is one of conformity. It is quite another thing, however, to suppose that this relation is what constitutes the truth of knowledge.

For we must take account of the fact that the mind's conformity with being is itself known whenever there is knowledge. This is not a new discovery. The only thing that is new is our admitting it into our calculations concerning the nature of truth. But Saint Thomas, for example, remarked upon it, noting that truth

> . . . may be in the sense, or in the intellect [simply apprehending, in the same way in which truth is said to be] in a true thing [namely, in a secondary sense of the term]; but it is not [in the sense, or in the simple apprehension of the intellect, in an

[9] Nicolas Berdyaev, *The Destiny of Man,* New York, Harper & Row, Publishers, Harper Torchbook, 1959, pp. 1-2.

> intentional way, that is] in the way in which the known is in the knower, as is required by that which we [properly] call truth; for the perfection of the intellect is truth as known.[10]

But Saint Thomas put this observation to no other use than to conclude, somewhat unfortunately, that truth is found only in the judgment. However, if we take account of the *experience* of truth in order to understand what truth is, then we may note that the mind's relation of conformity with being, when it knows truthfully, does not warrant the assumption that this conformity itself expresses the nature of truth "in itself," independently of our understanding of it, by virtue of what truth is prior to its coming into being in knowledge. For this would amount to assuming that the truth of the judgment, "Truth is the conformity of the mind with being," consists in the mind's conformity with its own *pre-cognitive* relation to the object of knowledge. Conversely, the classical concept of truth *presupposes* that the conformity of the mind with its object, which *supposedly* results from the act of knowledge, is warranted by a relation of opposition between the mind and its object *prior to knowledge*. The difficulty should be obvious: this would construe true knowledge as literally a *re-cognition* of what is, *prior to a cognition* of it. Yet, it is this very assumption which permits a philosopher like Saint Thomas to ignore the fact that "The perfection of the intellect is truth as known" when it comes to defining truth.

In other words, the conformity of the mind with being can be asserted either from the viewpoint of immediate experience or else from a viewpoint which, by abstraction, supposes itself to be outside experience. The latter alternative makes it possible to define truth as the conformity of the mind with being—but it yields a strictly *a priori* definition of truth, a definition which is not warranted by experience or able to withstand criticism, because it is grounded on an assumption which is contrary to fact. For the supposition that we may abstract from experience in order to examine experience is contrary to fact: it assumes that we can stand outside immediate experience in order to judge empirically the conformity (or nonconformity) of two things foreign to us, namely, subject and object. The former alternative, on the other hand, grounds the mind's

[10] Thomas Aquinas, *Summa Theologiae*, I, 16, 2.

conformity with being upon experience—but it implies that truth cannot be defined as the mind's conformity with things. In a nutshell: the classical conception of truth and the infallibility of the intellect involve each other. If the reality of error is acknowledged, or if the empirical character of truth is maintained, no epistemology could define truth as the conformity of the intellect with things. For to define it so would be to define it *a priori* from a viewpoint external to the intellect itself.[11]

Again, those who define truth as the conformity of mind with being forget that this definition must itself be judged to be true. Yet, on the classical assumption of truth, this judgment can never be made. Therefore, either we uncritically assume that the classical definition of truth is true, or else we judge it so strictly *a priori*. This is therefore a precritical conception of truth, corresponding with a precritical conception of knowledge. If, on the contrary, the truth of our knowledge of the nature of truth is to be empirically grounded, it is necessary to take account of the empirical nature of truth. The conformity of mind with being is an empirical fact; it exists in experience; it is itself known. Hence, whenever we observe this conformity, truth has *already* come into being. The conformity in question cannot therefore be a fact of nature, a fact

[11] This procedure might be temporarily defended by resorting to the idea that the truth of such a definition of truth was itself the conformity of the mind (in the act of asserting the definition of truth) with that reality which is the world of God's creation (that is, the totality of man and nature). In other words, the truth of our understanding of truth is the conformity of the intellect with the state of affairs established by God, namely, a world in which the intellect and things face each other, are spatially and temporally related, and act transitively upon each other. The precognitive relation of mind to things is the *divinely established* relation that obtains in a world of natures within which man, a being who is capable of knowing such a relation, has been placed.

Thus, the failure to take account of the empirical character of truth is conditioned by the assumption that the definition of truth as conformity of the mind with things is made from the viewpoint of someone who is above both the human mind and its objects—and God, who has established both, and the relations between them, is the only being who *in reality*, and not merely fictitiously (as is the case with man himself), corresponds with this description. The nature of this asumption did not rise to the surface as long as the problematic character of the classical concept of knowledge remained likewise submerged. But when the Cartesian problem emerged, the assumption was unearthed. Descartes' appeal to the veracity of God was but the logical outcome of the doctrine of Saint Thomas.

whose truth has been apprehended from a third viewpoint external to both mind and being. The conformity follows upon it. But it cannot be what truth *is*.

Evidently, the truth which *is* is that which is the basis of the logical relation of conformity of mind with being. In this view, the truth of knowledge is essentially of the order of *being*. And since truth is the achievement or fulfillment of knowledge, it must be conceived as the being of knowledge, the being of mind. Moreover, if we recall that knowledge produces the opposition of subject and object, we may further conclude that truth is the being of the knowing being, man, as the self emerges by differentiation from the nonself or, in other words, by the objectification of being. Therefore, the mind's relation of conformity with being, which results from true knowledge, is a conformity with being precisely insofar as being is objectified by knowledge.

This conformity is not grounded upon the respect due, as it were, to the supposedly prior claims of being over man. All metaphors which indicate any sort of "submission" of the mind to reality—a submission, indeed, sometimes said to be due in humility—are radically mistaken and misleading. It is not, of course, that there would be anything shameful in such submission, any more than there would be anything meritorious in it. It would seem indeed more in keeping with the scientific, empirical character of epistemology to conceive the mind's relation to reality in strictly nonhierarchical terms, in the absence of all *a priori* preoccupations with superiority-inferiority, with veneration or *amour propre*, with moral right or wrong. These considerations may follow. But to begin with, the empirical facts are in themselves neither virtuous nor immoral, neither proud nor meek, neither anal-erotic nor sado-masochistic—but simply, as best we can determine it, a matter of fact.

The mind's conformity with being, then, is not what we should procure; it is not what we should strive for. It is understandable if in this respect we have been the victims of a confusion not unlike that of a doting mother who would force her child to wear eyeglasses, because a scientific survey had revealed that most geniuses had bad eyesight beginning in childhood. We are now in a position to understand that the mind's conformity with being has a role within the process of man's quest for truth, that is, man's quest for creatively being himself—even if this role is almost precisely the opposite of what we have taken it to be. For in a sense, the mind's conformity with being, insofar as it manifests the truth of knowledge, is what impels the intellect to transcend its own truth; the mind's conformity with being is there to be *overcome*, to be the point of transition from truth to truth. It is not to be understood, therefore, as a conformity with what *already* was, or a conformity with what *forever* will continue to be. It is a conformity with what is; it is at once the sign that we have come to the truth and the sign that the truth is yet to come. It is not a passive but a creative relation, which began with what used to be, but which even now is being altered—reconceptualized, revised, and refashioned—by the self-creative consciousness of man in order that it may become itself.

But this is not the occasion to expand on the creativity and developmental character of truth. We must rather reflect upon the implications of these notions for our understanding of the nature of error.

The inadequacy of the classical concept of error may now be apparent. Heidegger has called attention to the etymology of the word, which points to our thinking of error as a sort of wandering, a straying from the path. But Heidegger seems to accept to some extent the fundamental validity of this metaphor, merely transposing it from the logical to the ontological order:

> Man errs. He does not merely fall into error, he lives in error always because by ex-isting, he in-sists and is thus already in error. The error in which he lives is not just something that runs along beside him like a ditch, something he occasionally falls into. No, error is part of the inner structure of *Da-sein,* in which historical man is involved.[12]

For all its truth, this view seems to me to err in the opposite direction of Thomism. Though it rightly recognizes the ontic reality of error, it fails to realize its strictly relative nature to truth. The metaphor of "error," the mind going astray, is fundamentally invalid if there is no predetermined path which knowledge is required to tread, no truth predetemined by an *a priori* disposition such as a

[12] Martin Heidegger, "The Essence of Truth," *Existence and Being,* ed. Werner Brock, tr. Douglas Scott *et al.*, London, Vision Press, 1949, pp. 344-345.

"pre-established harmony" implicit in God's creation of both the mind and its objects. For there is no empirical reason whatever to suppose that, prior to the truth of knowledge, there is a truth of things, constituted by God's knowledge of things, which is the measure of the truth of human knowledge.

But if knowledge has truth value insofar as it is an achievement of the order of being rather than a retracing of a path previously mapped out, then error is not a deviation from a prescribed standard. It is not a failure to discover what we are prerequired to discover, but a failure of consciousness to achieve itself—a failure which, of course, admits of wide variations in degree. Error is thus strictly relative to truth, and vice versa. It is a real and intrinsic part of knowledge. Quite as Heidegger said, man "does not merely fall into error, he lives in error. . . ."

It is necessary to add, however, that man lives in error in the same way and at the same time that he lives in truth. There is no erroneous knowledge which does not at least point in the direction or open up the possibility of truth. Conversely, as long as consciousness is in the process of development, there is no truth so true that we may discard the possibility that in the future its relative error might come to light. Likewise, this understanding of error helps explain why there can be some *truly false* knowledge—that is, why there can be knowledge which is truly knowledge, yet is not true knowledge but false. Indeed, insofar as it is not yet achieved, is not yet fully itself, true knowledge is truly knowledge and yet is always short of the truth.

This makes sense of the retrospective character of error. We can never experience *being* mistaken; we can experience only *having been* mistaken. But we should beware of two closely connected misinterpretations of this fact. (1) The experience of *having been* mistaken means that at an earlier time we *were* in error and simply failed to realize it. We tend to assume that we might have been aware of being in error at an earlier time—that there is therefore no special significance to the fact that error is always experienced retrospectively, and it may well be that in the future we will experience *being* in error. (2) The experience of *being* in the truth means that we will never come to think that we were in error unless in fact we *are* in error now but somehow have failed to realize it. But if we have failed to realize it this time, we might well realize it on the next occasion (see misinterpretation 1). The combination of (1) and (2) spells dogmatism and intolerance.

It seems more reasonable to suppose that we *cannot* experience being (at present) in error, but only being (at present) in the truth—and that this is indicative of the nature of knowledge and of the nature of error and truth. The retrospective character of error is but the converse of the prospective character of truth. For the truth in which we *are*, if we are aware of the real possibility of error even though we are not experiencing it at all, must be conceived as that which we *pursue*. Unless we interpret it dogmatically, as above, the experience of truth is the experience of that which lies before us and beckons. Thus, the very truth of experience points beyond itself—above all by creating suspicion about itself, by opening up the possibility of supposing itself to be false. Conversely, error is that which we wish to avoid, that which the truth must be purified from. In the pursuit of truth, we can be held back by retaining erroneous knowledge or by not transcending true knowledge—and we can be impelled forward by transcending erroneous knowledge as well as by giving up the true knowledge we already have.

Error, then, is not an abnormal, abortive issue of knowledge; it is a normal condition of its development. "To err is human," not particularly, as Pope thought, in the sense that it is forgivable, but in the sense that in the normal run of human affairs, it seems to be the ordinary way in which we learn and progress in the truth. The idea that unless its natural course is impeded, the human intellect will uninterruptedly and without error progress from not-knowing to knowing is unrealistic and self-deceptive to the point of presumption. This unwarranted optimism, moreover, is the cause of an unwarranted pessimism in the face of the reality of error. If we conceive the intellect as essentially infallible, we are bound to be intolerant of error. All this begins to come about when we fail to accept the facts of experience about experience itself, and proceed instead to define truth in terms of what presumably it ought to be, rather than what it in fact can be *experienced* to be.

If, on the contrary, we are resolved to ascertain the nature of truth from what we observe about it, we are likely to admit that error has a most important and valuable role in the emergence of truth. The creative, developmental character of human knowledge means that the quality of its possible achievement is proportional to the quality of its possible failure. We cannot reasonably expect human knowledge to progress without making mistakes. What we may reasonably though by no means infallibly expect is that if we keep making mistakes, we will in the end make some progress in the pursuit of truth. Conversely, we can forbid ourselves the possibility of error only by denying ourselves the cultivation of truth. Thus, it is better—I mean, it is more natural, more in accordance with the nature of human knowledge—to err than to remain ignorant, to err than to allow the truth to stagnate, to err than to forego the development of consciousness, to err than to risk the neglect of truth. The implications of this view for the question of academic freedom may be easily surmised.

The question may be raised at this point, however, whether the above observations may apply *only* to knowledge—whether the truth of faith must not be exempted from all conclusions about that truth which is relative to error, on the grounds that the truth of faith is of divine Provenance and therefore admits of no relation to error.

Let us beware of a possible confusion between the divinity of the "object" of man's belief and the humanity of belief in God. For all its "supernatural" character, faith is a type of experience, and cannot as such be excluded from the canons of experience. Faith is a reality of the same phenomenal order as every other experience. On the other hand, it is a *peculiar* type of experience. Religious experience is unique in that it plays a transforming role in relation to all other experience. For faith gives meaning to every other experience. Indeed, as Brian Wicker has pointed out, faith is the fundamental meaningfulness of ordinary experience. For instance, to integrate faith and experience is nothing else than to interpret experience truthfully, to derive the truth from experience: "The problem is that of finding an intellectual basis upon which to understand the meanings which this world offers us. This is the first priority—not the imposition of Christianity . . . but the discovery of a new kind of intelligibility." [13] This is why it is legitimate to

[13] Brian Wicker, *Toward a Contemporary Christianity*, Notre Dame, Ind., University of Notre Dame Press, 1967, p. 262.

speak of faith *and* experience, at the same time that we strive toward an *integration* of the two (notwithstanding the "supernatural" quality of one and the "natural" quality of the other). In reality we find not experience *and* faith but experience and its religious dimension.

Hence, such formulas as Brian Wicker's need not imply that faith (that is, religious experience) is reducible to nonreligious, "secular," or "natural" experience. Quite the contrary, the point is that ordinary human experience is *insufficient* unto itself unless it extends itself into a new, extraordinary dimension. When it so extends itself, experience becomes *religious* experience, or faith. Thus, the apparent opposition between faith and experience means simply this: precisely insofar as experience is immanent in the being of man, experience has a transcendent dimension, namely, faith. But faith transcends experience only because it is the transcendence *of* experience. Faith does not transcend experience by ceasing to be experience. Faith is simply that which gives ultimate meaning to ordinary human experience. Faith is the meaning, yet to be realized, of that which *already* exists, namely, experience.

In this context, however, *ultimacy* should not carry the Hellenic connotation of *finality*. All it means is this: experience as such already exists, but unless we understand it as in the classical tradition, experience must be understood as a participation in being and not as a reduplication of it. But if so, the experience which *already* exists clamors for a meaningfulness which it can only find *beyond itself*. I do not mean: beyond experience altogether. This would be a contradiction in terms. I mean: beyond experience insofar as experience *already* is.

The "projective" character of human consciousness is thus to be understood neither in terms of the exclusively moral existence of man (as if the distinction between the cognitive rational faculty and the appetitive rational faculty were valid) nor as a paradoxical attribute of human freedom (as if the gift of a totally indeterminate future which we must indeed create were a condemnation willy-nilly to choose freedom without becoming free). For man is not a thinking *and* willing substance. He is the being who comes into being, the being who emerges as such through self-differentiation from being. He is therefore being conscious of itself. Man is being present to itself. Well, faith is precisely the transcendent, projective dimension of the presence of human consciousness to itself.

Thus conceived, the life of the intellect requires freedom not only, as we have previously seen, of its very nature and for its proper perfection but *above all* by virtue of its religious vocation and commitment, for its proper perfection as the life of a *believing* intellect. Intellectual freedom is not a side effect of the freedom of the person, the converse would be closer to the truth. And intellectual freedom is not any the less required because faith perfects the intellect; the contrary would be closer to the truth.

Saint Thomas thought that the intellect inevitably progresses in its acquisition of the truth unless disorder due to sin interposes itself. In his view, faith is in part a remedy for the "darkness" of the fallen intellect. But it would be more accurate to say that growth in the truth is an intrinsic, natural possibility which requires for its actuality the free creativity and initiative of the mind. In this view, faith is in part the normal (not to say "natural") outcome of the emergence of consciousness.[14] Therefore, whatever facilitates the emergence and development of the truth of faith implies of its very nature the risk of error. Conversely, to void this risk is to forbid the possible development of the truth to which we are *religiously* committed, if not also to undermine it and to sap its inner life.

It need hardly be stressed that intellectual freedom is due not only to the individual believer in relation to his intellectual community, but in the very first place to that community in relation to the Church as a whole. It is not only for the benefit of the individual but as much for that of the Christian academy that the academic freedom of individuals should be preserved. Likewise, the academic freedom of the academy must be preserved not only for the academy's sake but for that of the whole Church. For the

[14] Edward Schillebeeckx says: "Being present to oneself, self-awareness is therefore in the last analysis religious, is inescapably a religious act. Thus human existence does not leave man the choice to be *not*-religious: he is forced by his own being to be religious or irreligious, to love or to disavow his own being; and in both cases it is a question of a religiously relevant action. To stand before oneself is to stand before God." ("Faith and Self-understanding," in T. Patrick Burke, ed., *The Word in History,* New York, Sheed & Ward, 1966, p. 49).

Christian academy best serves the interests of the Church when it freely devotes itself to the cultivation of the intellect and the promotion of inquiry. The Christian academy that restricts the academic freedom of its members or renounces its own has abdicated its responsibilities to the Church.

It should be noted, then, that insofar as it can be said to be a *right*, academic freedom is not the right to maintain particular views against general consensus. It is the right to *participate*, discharging one's vocation, in the common task of the Christian community. Likewise, the academy as a whole has the right, correlative with a duty, to participate in the growth and development of the truth of faith which belongs to the Church as a whole.

If epistemological considerations do not move those who may continue to be frightened by the possibility of error, a pragmatic appeal might be made to historical experience. The last hundred years of the history of the Church have shown with unprecedented clarity the imprudence of casting out dissent. Nothing so facilitates the proliferation of error and the stagnation of the intellect as enforced conformity, which automatically rewards inertia, myopia, passivity, uncreativity, and mediocrity. Who can be aware of recent history and yet fail to agree that the consequences of several generations of internal intellectual intolerance in the Church are painfully surfacing today? Intolerance is not even efficient. In the end, it never really succeeds in preventing error. Worse yet, sometimes it makes error all the more insidious if it is unacknowledged, and renders it all the more deceptive if it is hidden under the self-delusion of truth.

On the other hand, perhaps the whole of the postconciliar unhappiness of the Church is not an excessive price to pay to Clio if she will really teach us the lesson that the Christian academy is not a society for the preservation of past truth and the avoidance of future error, but a collective Christian endeavor freely dedicated to the cultivation of truth—an end to which it converts all it possesses, including, upon occasion, error itself.

Contributors

Contributors

KATHARINE T. HARGROVE, R.S.C.J., is associate professor of religion at Manhattanville College, Purchase, New York. She has contributed articles to the New Catholic Encyclopedia and to various periodicals including *Worship*, *Catholic Mind*, and *Cross and Crown*; her book reviews have appeared in *Bible Today*, *Religious Education*, *Living Light*, and *Theological Studies*. In 1966, after publication of *The Star and the Cross* (Bruce Publishing Company), Sister Hargrove received the Edith Stein Award. Currently, she is serving as a member of the Executive Committee of the Secretariat for Catholic-Jewish Relations.

RABBI EUGENE B. BOROWITZ, currently professor of education and religious thought at Hebrew Union College–Jewish Institute of Religion in New York City, is also visiting lecturer in contemporary Jewish thought at the Jewish Theological Seminary of America. He is the author of *A Layman's Introduction to Religious Existentialism*, editor of B'nai B'rith's new adult education series entitled *The Jewish Sources Speak*, and editorial adviser to Behrman House Publishers, and he contributes essays and book reviews to such organs as the quarterly *Judaism* and the *Journal of the Central Conference of American Rabbis*.

SISTER MARY PIERCE BUTLER, M.S.B.T, received her master's degree in religious education from Catholic University, and is at present a candidate for a doctorate in theology at Fordham University. An article published in *Worship* (April, 1963) which asks "Must We Teach Morality According to the Decalogue?" indicates the impact of *aggiornamento* on the author of the chapter dealing with "The Relevance of Biblical Language to Theology" which is included in this issue of *On the Other Side.*

REV. WILLIAM J. BYRON, S.J., at present assistant professor of economics at Loyola College in Baltimore, held a research fellowship at the University of Maryland, where he obtained his doctorate in economics. Prior to this he had been awarded graduate degrees from St. Louis University and Woodstock College, where he was ordained to the priesthood in 1961. The variety of his interests is indicated by a spate of articles in *America, Catholic Mind, Harvard Business Review,* and *Mergers and Acquisitions,* among other publications.

REV. PAUL L. CIOFFI, S.J., completed his philosophical and theological studies at Woodstock College, and then studied at the International Center for Studies in Religious Education (Lumen Vitae) in Brussels, receiving its diploma in 1962. From 1962 to 1964, he taught undergraduate courses in theology at Georgetown University. A dynamic participant in diocesan catechetical workshops and institutes, he is now a doctoral candidate in the School of Religious Education at Catholic University.

LEONARD G. CLOUGH was ordained to the ministry in the United Church of Christ in 1944. He has been campus pastor of the First Church in Cambridge, Massachusetts; executive secretary of the New England Student Christian Movement; and pastor of the Church of Christ at Dartmouth College. Since 1963, he has been general secretary of the University Christian Movement and assistant director of the Department of Higher Education, National Council of the Churches of Christ in the U. S. A. He serves on committees for fair housing and civic unity, and contributes articles to various church journals.

LESLIE DEWART is associate professor in the Department of Philosophy at St. Michael's College, University of Toronto. The author of *Christianity and Revolution* and *The Future of Belief,* and associate editor of *Continuum,* Dr. Dewart is widely known because of his contributions to *The Future of Belief Debate,* currently a popular topic. His writings are also to be found in *Contraception and Holiness, The Prospect of Change, Brief to the*

Bishops, Peace on Earth: The Way Ahead, and *The New Morality: Continuity and Discontinuity.*

EDWARD J. FOYE, chairman of the theology department at Trinity College in Washington, D. C., has been managing editor of *Front Line* since its inception in 1962. At various times he has been associate editor for Newman Press, editor-in-chief of Helicon Press, associate editor of the Johns Hopkins Press, and managing editor of Herder and Herder. Author of many articles, Prof. Foye is at work on a study in the biblical theology of the sacraments to be entitled "The Dimensions of Christ in the Life of the Church."

SISTER M. REMBERT HUBING, O.S.F., chairman of the Art Department at Alverno College in Milwaukee, also teaches ceramics during summer sessions at Notre Dame University. In the academic year 1966-1967, her work was exhibited at Marquette University, the Biblical Liturgical Conference, the Ecclesiastical Exhibition, and South Dakota University and by the Wisconsin Designer Craftsmen and Traveling Wisconsin Designer. Winner of awards every year from 1957 through 1965 from the Wisconsin Designer Craftsmen, in 1966 she received one from Craftsmen U. S. A., the Museum of Contemporary Crafts.

REV. DANIEL C. MAGUIRE obtained his S.T.D. in 1959 from the Gregorian Institute in Rome. Returning to Philadelphia, he taught in the high school system there, and transferred later to Villanova University. From 1964 through 1966, he was professor of moral theology at Saint Mary's Seminary in Baltimore. At present he is associated with the Department of Religious Education at Catholic University in Washington, D. C.

REV. JAMES J. MEGIVERN, C.M., holds, in addition to earned degrees of S.T.L., S.T.D., and S.S.L., a D.D. (*honoris causa*) from Moravian Theological Seminary in Bethlehem, Pennsylvania, for his ecumenical work. His articles have appeared in *Scripture, The Ecumenist, America, One in Christ, Pax Romana Journal, Worship,* and *New Catholic Encyclopedia.* A member of the Columbia University Faculty New Testament Seminar, he is also chairman of the theology department at St. John's University in Jamaica, New York.

MOTHER ANGELITA MYERSCOUGH, AD.PP.S., not only obtained her doctorate in sacred history and Scripture from Catholic University of America but spent two years studying theology at Regina Mundi Institute in Rome. From 1962 until 1965, she was a member of the theology faculty of St. Louis University. Mother Angelita is currently on leave of absence from St. Louis University to serve as provincial superior of the Ruma province of her religious order.

MARY EILEEN PAUL taught theology for four years at Trinity College in Washington, D. C. She has contributed book reviews and articles to *Front Line*. Currently enrolled in the Th.D. program of the Graduate Theological Union in Berkeley, California, Miss Paul is at the same time working as director of studies in the Collegium of Unitas, a united campus ministry at Berkeley.

ROSEMARY RUETHER was elected a life member of the National Society for Religion in Higher Education in 1962. She had already been the recipient of a Danforth grant (1960-1961) before she accepted a Kent Fellowship (1962-1965). Dr. Ruether has had articles published in *The Saturday Evening Post*, *Reader's Digest*, *National Catholic Reporter*, *Jubilee*, *Commonweal*, *Christian Century*, and *The Ecumenist*. She is a lecturer in church history and theology at George Washington University and the School of Religion, Howard University.

M. RICHARD SHAULL is a graduate of Princeton Theological Seminary and recipient of a Guggenheim grant for the study of Latin American political ideologies. Prof. Schaull spent twenty years in South America as missionary, seminary professor, and university administrator. With Carl Oglesby, he wrote *Encounter with Revolution*, *Containment and Change*. He has written four volumes in Portuguese on Christian faith and social problems in addition to articles and chapters in various publications. In 1966, he was a speaker at the World Conference on Church and Society in Geneva.

RICHARD E. SHERRELL's nonteaching roles range from parish minister in Massachusetts and California to Danforth Campus Ministry grantee and assistant director, Department of Higher Education, National Council of the Churches of Christ in the